WIRE
YOURSELF
FOR
WEALTH

WIRE YOURSELF FOR WEALTH

Discover Your Personal
Money Profile to Effortlessly
Attract More Cash

LAURA LEIGH CLARKE

HAY HOUSE
Australia • Canada • Hong Kong • India
South Africa • United Kingdom • United States

First published and distributed in the United Kingdom by:
Hay House UK Ltd, 292B Kensal Rd, London W10 5BE.
Tel.: (44) 20 8962 1230; Fax: (44) 20 8962 1239.
www.hayhouse.co.uk

Published and distributed in the United States of America by:
Hay House, Inc., PO Box 5100, Carlsbad, CA 92018-5100.
Tel.: (1) 760 431 7695 or (800) 654 5126;
Fax: (1) 760 431 6948 or (800) 650 5115.
www.hayhouse.com

Published and distributed in Australia by:
Hay House Australia Ltd, 18/36 Ralph St, Alexandria NSW 2015.
Tel.: (61) 2 9669 4299; Fax: (61) 2 9669 4144.
www.hayhouse.com.au

Published and distributed in the Republic of South Africa by:
Hay House SA (Pty), Ltd, PO Box 990, Witkoppen 2068.
Tel./Fax: (27) 11 467 8904. www.hayhouse.co.za

Published and distributed in India by:
Hay House Publishers India, Muskaan Complex, Plot No.3, B-2,
Vasant Kunj, New Delhi – 110 070. Tel.: (91) 11 4176 1620;
Fax: (91) 11 4176 1630. www.hayhouse.co.in

Distributed in Canada by:
Raincoast, 9050 Shaughnessy St, Vancouver, BC V6P 6E5.
Tel.: (1) 604 323 7100; Fax: (1) 604 323 2600

Text and illustrations © Laura Leigh Clarke, 2012

The information given in this book should not be treated as a substitute for professional medical advice; always consult a medical practitioner. Any use of information in this book is at the reader's discretion and risk. Neither the author nor the publisher can be held responsible for any loss, claim or damage arising out of the use, or misuse, or the suggestions made or the failure to take medical advice.

A catalogue record for this book is available from the British Library.

ISBN: 978-1-84850-698-5

Printed and bound in Great Britain by TJ International, Padstow, Cornwall.

Contents

Acknowledgments

Special thanks firstly have to go to Guy 'Monkey' Rogerson for his endless support, optimism and encouragement. He has proven to be my biggest critic and greatest supporter. Thank you for tirelessly proofreading and being my sounding board well beyond the call of duty or reason.

Huge thanks must also go to my Mum and Dad, Trudy and Trevor Clarke, for encouragement by the bucket-load – with a healthy sprinkling of skepticism – and groundedness. Specifically thanks to Dad for always being willing to challenge my 'woo-woo' thinking with interesting counter-arguments, tangents, and conversations on long horse-rides; and Mum for explaining everything and anything to me from before the time I could speak. It's thanks to her that I have grown up with the curiosity to seek deeper truths.

Many thanks must also go to the team at Hay House, for all their support, guidance, and continuing spirit of collaboration throughout the publishing process.

I would also like to extend my deep gratitude to Roger James Hamilton for permission to talk about his Wealth Dynamics profiling system for entrepreneurs. This is a phenomenal resource when pulling teams together and helping individuals to uncover their path of least resistance.

Special thanks also go to my friends and joint venture partners for the constant stream of challenge and inspiration to develop and test the concepts outlined in these pages. I look forward to many more workshops and ventures in the future.

Last and by no means least, I owe a debt of gratitude to all the incredible individuals who have come to me for coaching and workshops over the years. I have learned far more from them than they have from me. It is thanks to them constantly challenging me, stretching the boundaries of what is possible, and working through their situations that I have grown with them. Your successes are a constant source of inspiration, both to me and to those who follow in your footsteps. Thank you!

Introduction

Congratulations on taking action! You've taken the first step to wiring yourself for wealth. By reading this book you're giving yourself a gift: an opportunity to change your relationship with money for the better, for good.

If you're ready to make more money, with less effort and more spiritual zing, let's get started. The book is roughly divided into three parts. The first four chapters introduce you to the powerful concepts and ideas that we then build on later in the book. Chapter 5 focuses on how to embrace your inner Money Genius by discovering your Personal Wealth Profile, and how to use the strengths of that profile to your financial advantage. This chapter also covers how to engage others, bearing in mind that 'no person is an island,' as every success includes other people working toward a common vision. This section is quite strategic and practical. Then Chapters 6 through 9 of the book build on the skills we started to develop in the first four chapters. In this section we pull everything together and learn how to turbo-charge our results.

I have included practical exercises throughout the book. In my webinar courses, the individuals who achieved the most significant results and positive outcomes were those who took the time to complete the exercises. I constantly use the exercises within these pages to develop my own business and my vision for life. You will be amazed at the results you start to achieve if you set the time aside to do them and work honestly.

Some of the exercises are more challenging than others; if you find that many of the concepts I discuss in the book are new to you, you can skip the more advanced exercises to begin with. However, I heartily recommend that you go back through the book at a later date, and re-do the lessons and exercises – including the advanced ones – as this will allow you to gain the maximum benefit from the time you'll have already invested in the program.

Further, free resources are available on my website www.wireyourselfforwealth.com to assist you in achieving the results you truly desire. Please do take full advantage of them, as the audio programs, meditations, and guided releases are tools to really solidify the concepts explained in the book, and they will help you make the shift you seek.

To your success!

Laura Leigh Clarke

Chapter 1
Finding Your Money Mojo

Mojo: 'A charm or a spell', now more commonly used to mean 'sex appeal' or 'talent'; self-confidence; self-assuredness; a belief in the Self in any given situation.

Money Mojo: Your intrinsic ability to generate cash, money, and wealth, through living your purpose every day, following your passion, and manifesting the best life you can imagine... and ***allowing it all to fall into place, as if by magic***.

Imagine what your world would be like if you had all the money you needed all of the time, just by thinking about it. What might you choose to do? Where would you go? Who would you go with? What if you were completely free to do whatever you felt like doing, at any given time, without upsetting anyone or feeling you were being selfish?

Which burdens might you relinquish? What would you leave for someone else to do? Who would you call? Which calls would you avoid? What would you buy? What would you get rid of? What would you let go of?

Go ahead and take a few moments to contemplate what your life might be like if money was no object and you really were free to do whatever you chose. This is a useful and important exercise, because it sets our direction as we embark on the journey to wire ourselves for wealth.

After all, as you've probably already considered, while generating wealth includes the ability to make cash in the short term for survival (which we will discuss later), it is also a great deal more.

Unsticking the 'Stuckness'

The most common complaint I hear amongst working individuals, entrepreneurs, and would-be entrepreneurs is that they are sick and tired of feeling stuck. They are fed up with struggling and working hard only to make little progress. They are done with worrying about cash flow and chasing the next client. They are tired of showing up at industry seminars or logging on to Facebook and seeing everyone else apparently doing so much better – and it appearing easy for them.

But what if it didn't have to be this way? What if you could make great progress without all that struggle and effort? What if opportunities just dropped in your lap and progress was easy? What if it was as simple as taking the brakes off and making a few little adjustments to what you are already doing – then watching as these small actions have a massive impact on your results?

Sounds good? Well, what you are about to discover in these pages are the exact strategies that countless people have already employed to generate real-life results, effortlessly.

Meet Michael (this is not his real name – I have changed the names in this book to protect identities). Michael has a very successful business. He has a team of inspired and dedicated people who manage the ongoing work, leaving him free to channel his energy into expanding the business. He loves every aspect of what he does. Opportunities – which sometimes come from the unlikeliest places – just drop into his lap. Why? Because Michael is using his Money Mojo to live the life that lights him up.

But it wasn't always that way. There was a time when he was clinically depressed. His business partner was making dubious deals behind his back and was trying to steal away the company's clients. His contractors were unreliable and the business was on the verge of bankruptcy. He was also simultaneously managing two lawsuits that had been dragging on for years: one against someone who had been bullying him; the other to take possession of a house he rightfully owned. Michael's life read like something out of a soap opera, except that it was really happening and he was the only one who could turn it around.

And he managed to do just that: his company went from near bankruptcy to a turnover of $3.3m (£2.2m) in less than twelve months! So how did he do it? He decided to follow the strategies outlined in this book – and he still uses them to this day.

And Michael is not alone. As you will discover as you read on, countless other people have used these methods to generate the very results you personally may be trying to produce. So my first message to you is: If they can do it, so can you!

I have broken down my wealth-creating strategies into seven key steps, which we will explore in detail in the rest of the book. What these seven strategies will show you is that no matter who you are, and where you are financially, you already have within you everything you need in order to become a fabulous success. They will help you unlock those abilities and chip away the resistance that is preventing you from being all you would choose to be.

You may have noticed how sometimes you just can't get something to work, no matter how hard you try. Even though you may be doing everything right, you still seem to end up back at square one, a little bit more tired and a little less willing to try again. Does this sound familiar? This scenario happens when you are trying to plough forward with the brakes on. By brakes I mean the internal inertia that can hold you back, a kind of internal resistance. You need to overcome this inertia if you want to succeed. This resistance, which drains you and makes you feel tired, confused, and unable to manifest the results you choose, is the result of what, from now on, we will refer to as *baggage*.

Often it's *emotional baggage*, wrapped up in the corresponding *energetic baggage* you may not even be aware of right now. However, if you're able to identify your baggage and let it go, you will find you become lighter and lighter. And the lighter you become, the more energy you will have for creating the results you choose, and the more effortless the whole process will be for you. Don't worry if you don't yet know how to identify your baggage and let it go, as we tackle this subject in depth in Chapter 3. You will learn precisely how to rid yourself of all this baggage, and be free of it forever. By releasing this baggage, you will find that everything will naturally become more and more effortless. And living the dream – that distant reality you contemplated when I asked you at the beginning of this chapter what you would do if you were free to do whatever you chose – becomes a much closer possibility.

I mentioned above that Michael used his Money Mojo. What exactly is Money Mojo? Michael had tapped into what I call the 'Money Genius' in his brain and had managed to implement some massive changes to generate some very positive results. What you may not yet realize is that you, too, have a Money Genius – perhaps a Warren Buffett, a Richard Branson, a Donald Trump, or a Lady Gaga – sitting in the corner of your mind. If you're not yet making the money you would love to make, the likelihood is that your Money Genius is lying dormant – metaphorically sitting on the sofa, flicking through TV channels, and not knowing what to tune in to.

You can find out what your Money Genius might be through a process called *profiling*, which we will be exploring later (see Chapters 4 and 5). Profiling is a method in which an individual takes a test, like a questionnaire. The results can then be analysed according to known statistical data and interpreted to give greater insight – in this case – into the person's most effective way to make money. Once you discover what your profile is, your Mojo is released and your Money Genius knows exactly what to tune in to. All of a sudden making money becomes straightforward and you wonder why on earth you have been finding it so tough!

This is also the magic moment when you get into your natural Flow. You know – that place where everything is fun, easy, and effortless. Flow is a state in which events conspire to help you, so that you make progress easily and produce results as if you had a magic wand. Now you've probably experienced times when things just slotted into place: you were in the right place at the right time; chance acquaintances randomly chose to assist you and point you in the right direction; and you found the tasks at hand so easy, you felt like a master. This is Flow, when your Mojo is at its maximum.

Flow could also be defined as a series of perfect moments, joined seamlessly up together, one after another. You will find it much easier to be in Flow when you know your Money Genius type because then you can implement the wealth strategies that work best for your personality.

By the end of this book, I will also share with you the one thing that is holding you back the most. This is the most controversial thing I ever suggest in my coaching and training. And it's the one thing that people almost certainly argue about when I first suggest it. But it is also always the one thing that, once accepted, enables them to make massive – and I mean absolutely ENORMOUS – shifts in their businesses. This is the one thing you *must* do if you are to master the seven strategies to wire yourself for wealth.

So buckle up – life is about to flow.

Your Vehicle of Value Conversion

Dreams are great, but in order to generate cash doing what you love, you need a vehicle through which to pull the cash into your bank account. This is where your Vehicle of Value Conversion comes in.

Every person, including you, has an innate value. I'm talking about a very specific, intrinsic value, a gift that you have to give to the world. This value is your own special blend of talents and qualities and it's for you to discover and understand it. There are clues you leave behind as to what this innate value is. They are right there in the projects you've already succeeded at, as well as in those that didn't go so well.

A good way to get an indication of where someone's gift lies is to ask them what occupies their thoughts and time, and what they would continue to do even if they weren't being paid to do it. Your task is to see each project or business you undertake as a playground in which to uncover more and more of your innate value. The clever part is then to harness that value for the benefit of the business, and then later for the good of humankind. There is a shortcut to discovering the 'flavor' of your blend of talents and abilities, which we will explore when we talk about wealth profiling (see Chapters 4 and 5), but you'll still need to undertake some self-reflection on this topic.

Within this vehicle, within the time you have on this particular project, you will have challenges to overcome, successes to celebrate, parts of your personality to work on, and wisdom to accumulate. If you step into each vehicle, not focusing simply on how much money you can make, but also looking at how you can grow as a person, you will quickly find your Flow and work out how to remain in it on an ongoing basis.

Now, let's zoom in a little on this vehicle. And as we do so, we realize that this innate value you carry within yourself needs an outlet in order to convert it into something of value in the physical world. This is your business.

Your business is the way in which you turn your own, unique intrinsic value into something the marketplace values – something that people will pay money for.

*Let me repeat – your business is the mechanism
you use to convert your innate value into cash.*

It's a value extraction device, if you like. This means that your best chance of success lies in extracting whatever your biggest value is, and unleashing it directly onto the marketplace. And this is why I call your business your Vehicle of Value Conversion: The more value you deliver through your business, the more money people will pay you.

Scalability (the ability to handle a growing amount of work or to increase capacity to accommodate growth) is also important. The more scalability you have in getting your value out into the marketplace, the more profitable your business will be. This means that once you've discovered your Flow and worked out how to convert it into cash, you then need to focus on how to convert it into cash more quickly, more often, and in a scalable way.

This is where knowing your inner Money Genius comes in. There are eight Wealth Profiles – eight Money Genius types – that we will discuss in detail in Chapters 4 and 5. Your profile will be one of the eight and, whichever it turns out to be, it is an indication of the type (or 'flavor') of value you bring to a business. Your task is then to adopt the strategy for your profile in order to convert this value into cash.

It may be, for example, that your value lies not in creating a business or starting a project from scratch, but rather in contributing to one that already exists. In this case, you need to look at how you can add your Flow to the existing Flow and thus multiply the results of the efforts of the existing team.

Don't worry if you feel you haven't quite grasped everything we've covered so far. We'll be recapping this information and applying it to lots of situations throughout the book, so there will be plenty of opportunities for it to sink in. Just for now though, why not have a think about your own intrinsic value that you bring to the projects you are involved in.

What do you do that converts into cash? Jot down your answers below, as you'll need this information later. Also make a note as to whether or not you enjoy each task you list. For example, you may currently spend your time presenting your product or service to investors or to potential clients. Or you may make or manufacture something. Or then again you may have an admin role, organizing the orders that come in and making sure they go out on time. Or perhaps you do everything – if this is the case, note this down, too!

1. _____

2. _____

3. _____

4. _____

5. _____

6. _____

Now, which of those tasks do you really enjoy?

1. _____

2. _____

3. _____

4. _____

5. _____

6. _____

Be Still like a Mountain, But Flow like a River

I'd now like to share with you an example of how cash naturally follows when you do the things that light you up from the inside. It's simply not the case that you have to do something that's dull and hard work in order to make money.

Let me tell you briefly about Claire, who wasn't rigid in her thinking at all. She came to me looking for guidance as to how to get out of a graphic design job she didn't particularly enjoy, so that she could make more of the Pilates classes she was teaching.

Based on her Money Genius type we realized that she wasn't working to her strengths in her graphic design job. But in her desired career change to teaching Pilates classes, she'd still be trying to perform against her natural talents and, worse still, the niche she was aiming for was massively over-saturated and underpaid. She was also frustrated at being unable to find, and keep, enough participants to make it worthwhile to run even a small number of Pilates classes.

Sometimes we need to step back and evaluate where we expect our value conversion to happen. We often expect it to come through a certain business venture in a certain way – so we focus our energy in the wrong direction, missing where the true value really lies. Claire was missing that her true profile, her Money Genius type, was really a Deal Maker who, as you will discover, is someone who is really good at bringing people and deals together. Such people are well known in their chosen field and their value lies in being able to extract value out of a contract between two or more parties for the mutual benefit of those involved. They're especially great at doing deals that magnify a person's or a product's presence, such as setting up new distribution channels.

Claire was thinking too small. Her best move was to step back from trying endlessly to fill her Pilates classes. Instead I suggested that she start to monitor everything happening in the mind-body-spirit niche in her locale. In doing this she would also be able to re-evaluate what she really wanted to do with her time, within a niche she was clearly attached to. She admitted almost immediately that she wasn't sure she wanted to run the Pilates classes full-time and that trying to fill the classes was hard work for her.

In time, she noticed that there was a gap in the market where she could add value. There were lots of people who had found a discipline such as Pilates or yoga and were open to experiencing more within the mind-body-spirit arena. Claire started building a cooperative of instructors, and massage and Reiki therapists, and pooled their databases. By making one big database she was able to provide each client with access to the other therapists and instructors at a reduced rate. Claire got to take a cut by running it for the good of everyone and the individual instructors increased the number of people on their books, too. And the clients of all the instructors and therapists were able to try new things.

In effect, Claire focused on a much bigger picture, which gave her much more opportunity to create wealth by taking a cut of the money changing hands. She now spends her time networking, meeting others, and getting to know individual trainers, therapists, and traders in the community – and she is loving every minute of it. Claire stood still like a mountain in her niche but flowed like a river to align herself with her natural Money Genius type.

Does This Mean She Sold Out?

No! Claire made a conscious decision to get out of a rut where she wasn't making money, and got into her Flow. It's not that she had to make a choice between doing what she loved and making money. She readily admitted that she wasn't sure that she wanted to spend all of her time running Pilates classes. She also confessed she wasn't that inspired by having to run it as a business, and much preferred do it as a hobby. But, by contrast, she loved putting people in touch with each other and getting to know new people, so she found the perfect solution by working with others in the mind-body-spirit professions.

And this brings us on to another important point: People often think that wealth and money are incompatible with spirituality and wonder how creating wealth fits into the mind-body-spirit field. Let's now take a closer look, as it's important we understand exactly what we mean by these concepts before we proceed further.

To Be Wealthy or to Be Spiritual... That Is the Question!

Or is it? In the subject area of wealth and finances, the most common misconception I come across is that to be wealthy is to be unenlightened, and that you can't be wealthy and spiritual at the same time.

I never did understand this, but people often quote the example of how they'd 'rather be spiritual than have a flash car'. Since when did being wealthy equate to having a flash car? And why can't you have wealth in financial terms *and* spiritual terms? Have you noticed how frequently people approach the subject of wealth with so many prejudices that they literally paralyze their own ability to take on board any helpful information before they give themselves a chance?

I started on the journey when I was 18. I moved to London for university, and happened upon the world of self-development. I attended all kinds of courses and events: wealth courses, trading courses, and NLP seminars. They all focused on mind-set and talked about the common wealth beliefs that stop people from having money. I was young and had not been exposed to these beliefs, so at that time I thought they were silly, but through the years I have come into contact with many people who do believe that *to be wealthy, you have to be 'unspiritual'*.

I was often confused when people said, 'Money is the root of all evil.' (This a misquote from the Bible, which in fact says, 'The *love* of money is the root of all evil.') I also didn't understand the saying 'Money doesn't grow on trees.' *So where does paper come from?* I would wonder, dismayed at the confusing logic and figures of speech these grown-ups used.

Do you identify with this attitude to money? The problem is that these are the very beliefs that are holding you back from having a decent amount of cash in the bank. They are simply socially accepted 'truths' with no real basis in reality, but if you cling to them, you will never be able to have the amount you desire. What is more, such beliefs will make it very easy for you to dismiss all the possibilities we're about to talk about as mumbo jumbo.

So I'm now going to address a few fundamental points briefly to help you if you're struggling with these specific culturally programmed beliefs. (We will return to this subject throughout the book, so that you will have a framework through which to release any other unhelpful beliefs around money.)

Let's return to the belief that a person cannot be spiritual and wealthy at the same time. Maybe you've already noticed this yourself, but I find that when my life expands in one area, it is naturally forced to expand in all other areas as well. It's as if the energy I'm putting into the one area causes a shift that automatically expands the other parts. I think of it as a balloon expanding when you breathe into it. It can't stay shriveled and small in some areas and still grow in others. Your life is the same. Perhaps you can intuitively see that if you expanded the spiritual area of your life, your financial life would automatically grow, too?

And vice versa – by sorting out your finances and increasing your wealth, you'd be making energetic shifts that would bring you to more profound spiritual understanding.

Yet I often come across individuals who are unable to let go of the belief that it's one or the other: wealth or spirituality. All the while they declare they are 'on the path' to becoming spiritually enlightened, whilst simultaneously complaining they earn a living doing a job they hate and only do it because they can't find anything better. This isn't spirituality, it's just hard work. This isn't freedom from desire, it's a prison of limitation... with a refusal to acknowledge the prison bars. It needn't be like this.

Another thing I've come to realize is that being able to take care of yourself is something you can't just 'transcend'. Transcending occurs when you've accumulated the wisdom to be learned from that particular phase and are able to move on. If you haven't mastered the basic ability to survive – to feed and clothe yourself – then you have no solid basis for higher evolution. Having someone lend you money or bail you out isn't demonstrating your ability to manifest in a positive way. It's saying 'I can only create when my survival is threatened.' This isn't transcending, it's skipping – you're just missing out a phase of spiritual development completely. And you're limiting yourself – cheating yourself out of true growth. But this kind of person isn't you. You're reading this because you already recognize that if you are to follow your true path, all aspects of your life must be in harmony, and that includes your ability to command your financial situation.

Wealth and Development of the Self

Wealth and personal development are intimately linked. If you don't develop the Self, even if you were handed a huge sum of money, the chances are you'd end up with the same amount of money you started with (or less) not long afterward.

The classic case for this is lottery winners. Did you know that over half of all lottery winners in the UK have lost all their money a mere 12 months after having a big win – greater than $1.5 million (£1 million) – and are in more debt than when they started? This is because psychologically they weren't wired to manage this kind of sum. They didn't energetically feel themselves worthy to have it. As a result, they inadvertently did everything they could to get rid of the cash, and keep it away from them!

You only have to Google the topic and read some of the stories in the online newspapers and you'll see what I mean. There are tales of people who gambled their money away; some who gave it away to anyone who asked; and others who spent it on hare-brained schemes that most of us would be skeptical of. There is even a story about a woman who won a huge amount, then borrowed more from a bank, using the monthly cheques from the lottery as collateral. When the lottery rules changed, allowing her to cash in her winnings in a lump sum, she did just that, and spent all of it without repaying the loan!

People who behave in this way when handling money are only following deep subconscious beliefs that they aren't worthy of having that money. As a result of their beliefs, they energetically attract into their experience circumstances and events that get them financially right back to zero, or worse, deep into debt.

And it's not just lottery winners who demonstrate this behavior. We all do it to various degrees. What happens when you get a little windfall of a few hundred dollars (pounds)? Do you invest it straight away? Or more likely do you use it to cover a few bills, or spend a little more at the supermarket one week, or use it to buy a pair of shoes, or something the kids have been clamoring for? It's okay to spend money – don't get me wrong. You've earned it. But if you're not already accumulating cash and assets, then it's likely you are doing similar things to the lottery winners: just pushing that extra cash away from you – albeit to a lesser degree, and perhaps in a less obvious and dramatic manner.

I recall in my early days of personal development listening to an audio recording of the inspirational speaker, Jim Rohn. He asserted that if the income ever exceeded the personal growth, then it would be very short-lived. He said that the only way to increase your financial worth is to develop your personal worth first. If you can relate to this, think about getting in place some kind of savings or investment account that you can continually add to when you make little unexpected gains above your normal income. Then you will be less tempted to just absorb it into your normally monthly spending. You'll have the beginnings of an organized financial strategy, which means that you will know what to do when you attract more money, and as a result you will be less resistant to letting it come to you. (You can check out the recommended reading section on page 225 for some more books on this topic.)

The other thing to realize about money is that having it is not going to make you an evil person! (You may giggle, but this is a common belief amongst normally sensible go-getters when they realize they are about to increase their income substantially.) Money only magnifies who you already are – it doesn't change you. If you can't manage your finances when you have a little, having a lot of money is only going to magnify the problems. Similarly, if you're a nice person already, having money isn't going to suddenly turn you into a monster!

You see we attract (and keep) the amount of money that we are comfortable with: money brings responsibility and different types of problems – for example, where to store it; how to allocate it to different projects; how much extra tax to pay; and whose advice to take. All these things can create emotional blockages that stop more money coming our way.

Building wealth machines (businesses, assets, and systems that generate money) and Vehicles of Value Conversion (those businesses and assets that convert your talents and skills into cash) comes with responsibilities, too. Take Bill Gates, the founder of computer giant Microsoft, as an example. If you had his wealth, you'd also have all the responsibilities of having that wealth, too – and you'd probably become so stressed out you'd be a wreck! Gates has allowed his relationship with money and wealth to evolve as his empire has grown. He would have had to develop as a person to be able to cope with the kinds of problems and responsibilities that would have cropped up in building Microsoft.

And it is the same for anyone who has ever amassed great wealth. So, remember what we said about allowing each project we undertake to be a playground? What if each project allowed you to become more and more comfortable with the responsibilities of having more cash? How about holding that in your mind as an intention as you go to work on your business?

It's All About Where Your Internal Wealth Thermostat Is Set

Another way of thinking about the amount of money we have is to see it as an internal 'Money Thermostat', which maintains the level we can comfortably handle. When we develop ourselves and get rid of our baggage, this thermostat goes up, meaning that we are now capable of coping with more wealth without becoming overwhelmed.

You can only go as fast as your internal thermostat will allow. It's not just lottery winners – everyone has this thermostat – and all we need to do is look around at the way we live, where we live, how much cash we have in our bank accounts, the value of our investments, and the wealth of the people we associate with on a regular basis to know exactly what level our thermostat is at.

The good news is that the seven keys, which I reveal in the chapters that follow, will show you how to raise this thermostat to whatever level you wish to achieve.

Wealth versus Money

One last thing to touch on before we start looking at the strategies in detail, is that there is indeed a difference between wealth and money. There is a tendency to use the two terms interchangeably – after all, if one wants more money, one often desires to be wealthy. In casual conversation we also accept that if someone has a lot of wealth, they have a lot of money. By the same token, we assume that if someone has a lot of money, they are wealthy. Let's be clear here. Money is cash or liquidity. It is our ability to buy, or spend, based on exchanging a common currency in whatever form that takes, whether it's physical pieces of colored paper or plastic cards, numbers in bank accounts or online transactions. Cash flows and money comes and goes.

Wealth, on the other hand, is what is left when all the money has gone. Roger Hamilton, the creator of Wealth Dynamics, the profiling system we will be using later, described this in terms of a garden. He says we should think of money as the butterflies, and people's money-making strategies as the people running around chasing the butterflies with nets. Some people have big nets; some have small ones; some are more effective or stealthier than others; but if you're chasing cash, you may as well be running around trying to catch butterflies in this highly inefficient way.

By contrast, if you cultivate and nurture a garden, you find that butterflies will naturally come and inhabit it in their hordes. What's more, there is no need to capture or take possession of a single butterfly – because they stay there all the time. Truly wealthy people have shown time and time again that they can lose all their money, and make it back in a heartbeat, because wealth isn't about the money. It's about cultivating a garden for the money to flow through.

So when generating wealth, build your garden. Nurture it. Fill it with all the things butterflies like. And in time, the garden will grow all on its own and effortlessly attract an endless supply of butterflies. To put it succinctly: Attract, don't chase.

One of the reasons people struggle and burn out when trying to make their fortune is that they run around trying to make money rather than being still and attracting the right money-making opportunities to them. What's more, part of the problem when we start is that we don't *trust* that money will come to us. But if we aren't resonating at the right energetic frequency it's because we don't have the confidence that we are worthy of attracting the opportunities. By the same token, simply waiting for it to happen won't help either. We have to trust that we will succeed and allow our success in.

One of the other things to be aware of when we're taking our initial steps toward true wealth is that there are so many courses and money-making schemes around, offering so many different strategies, and such diverse ways of chasing butterflies – for example, stock-market trading, internet marketing, affiliate marketing, property development, to name just a few – that we must beware of being bamboozled and overwhelmed.

So how do you know what's really the best path for you to take? How do you know that the strategy you are using is really the one that is going to create a luscious garden? How do you stop chasing and start attracting butterflies?

This is where the Wealth Dynamics Profile Test comes in (see Chapters 4 and 5), because it will help you discover which strategy you should be following given your precise personality profile. This is one of the seven keys that we will discuss in more detail in the chapters that follow.

This book is for the open-minded reader who is ready to make more money, has either a job or a business, or is self-employed, or is looking to embark on a new money-making venture. Though we will focus mostly on the responsibilities and actions of the individual, we will also cover the idea of building a team to provide any skills we don't have ourselves.

This applies whether you are a single individual working away at your passion, or an employee with a well-defined role. No matter what your circumstances, you are *never* an island. Other people are always going to be the bridge to your success, and as such you need to know how to attract the right people to help you, and how best to utilize the skills and flair they innately have. If you already run a business or manage a team, this goes without saying.

Points to Remember

- Making money shouldn't be a struggle

- Emotional baggage around money can be dropped, even if you've had it a long time

- Everyone has an intrinsic value

- Your business is the mechanism that converts your value into cash

- Focus on what you love and the tasks you enjoy

- You can be spiritual and wealthy at the same time. It's a choice.

So, how about we go ahead and start preparing the ground for that beautiful garden with the first key?

Chapter 2
Key 1: Increase Your Self-Esteem

In this chapter we are going to talk about your secret ally in getting your Money Mojo in full swing! With just this one thing, in its raw form, you will be able to single-handedly transform your finances, and become a total money magnet. Not only that, but combine this secret ingredient with your Vehicle of Value Conversion (see page 6) and guess what...? ...You'll boost your money magnetism into the stratosphere – and that's a promise!

I have seen my own coaching clients work on just this one thing and they go from being stressed out and anxious over their job to being completely peaceful and productive. I have seen individuals go from being at the mercy of their to-do list, to being able to stand back and just do the stuff that brings in the super-results... and cash! I have also seen business owners go from fretting about negative cash flow, to having a situation where their focus is on great customer service and the cash flow takes care of itself.

So what is this magic secret ingredient, I hear you ask? It's *self-esteem*. Unless you have good, solid self-esteem the other keys to unlocking your Money Mojo will do little for you. Without this one crucial thing, it's like tossing a beautiful, vital, quick-growing seed onto lifeless concrete. It won't grow.

This one thing has been quietly determining your level of wealth in the background, all your life. But your dreams and goals deserve the best chance to flourish. I'm now going to show you how this one thing will maximize your chances of success, and how you can develop it on demand.

Having worked with clients from a variety of backgrounds I have found that we are never able to create more wealth in our lives until we feel truly worthy of having all the wonderful things in life. Working on anything else, such as business strategies or mind-sets, doesn't seem to have much effect until we feel worthy of having more. It's almost as if our internal thermostats are set too low and our inner compasses are constantly readjusting, leaving us in a constant state of struggle and confusion – a tough place to be.

Cultivating adequate self-esteem is the very first thing to tackle when we decide to embark on a journey to attract more wealth. Without it, we don't deem ourselves worthy of having anything of value, because we don't see ourselves as *being* anything of any value. And if that's what we think, feel, and resonate, then that is exactly what we are going to attract into our reality.

The great news is that we *can* work on our self-esteem to create massive shifts in our ability to create and attract wealth. Wealth, after all, is just a reflection of the amount of value we contribute to the outside world. The more value we can provide to others, the more they deem us worthy of receiving their hard-earned cash in exchange for that value. However, if we don't value ourselves, there is no way we will ever allow anyone else to value us. Others around us are very good at following our lead, so if we place little value on ourselves they, in turn, will place the same amount of worth on us.

You see, when we meet people they can get a sense of us before we even say a word. This is more than simply body language. It's energy language. Every interaction with another person involves our energy systems butting up against each other. These energy systems exchange huge amounts of information – even though we may not be saying very much to each other. And yes, most of this information exchange is unconscious. Haven't you noticed when you meet someone that you can very quickly get a sense of who they are?

Well, they know exactly who you are, too. And if your energy system is saying: 'Boy am I broke! I really need your business,' you're inadvertently going to be pushing them away. Conversely, when we truly value ourselves – and I mean *genuinely* – and we are not just pretending in order to compensate for our lack of self-esteem, we free others to see us as we really are. All of a sudden our market value increases exponentially and effortlessly. I say 'effortlessly' because once our true self-esteem is in place we become centered and magnetic, and the rest falls naturally into place.

At the end of this chapter I will introduce you to some exercises that will not only help you increase your self-esteem, but also show you how to keep it at a high level.

Why Does Creating Wealth Suddenly Become So Much Easier?

It's like our garden we referred to earlier. Once we have fertile ground, growing whatever plants we choose becomes relatively easy. Okay, so we may need to make some adjustments and introduce the seeds or saplings, but that's the easy part. The important thing is that we have fertile ground. And, as an astute reader, you are probably also thinking about weeds. In fertile ground weeds may indeed flourish, so they will need to be uprooted, which is much easier to do when the earth is moist and tilled rather than hard and dry, as it was before we started to prepare it. What's more, you are in a position of choice – you can *choose* precisely which plants you allow to grow and flourish, and which you uproot immediately.

How Is It that Self-Esteem Has Such a Massive Effect?

By raising your level of self-worth you are affecting your entire energy field. As I've already mentioned, most of the information we communicate to each other is through our energy fields and so, if you have genuinely high self-regard, this shines through. Moreover, more of who you *truly are* shines through and people (either consciously or subconsciously) pick up on this.

You'll probably have noticed how some people you meet just exude power. They're grounded and centered. Without being harsh or forceful, they just seem to command a certain respect. Once you increase your self-esteem you'll also notice how you shift your energetic systems to accommodate this. You may start to respond to the same situations differently, with more confidence and maturity. Others will automatically treat you better and enjoy your presence. They'll value your opinion and your jokes (even the lame ones!) and, of course, they'll increase what they are willing to exchange for the value you bring to them in the form of your products and services.

What Is This Energy Field We Keep Referring to?

You have a physical body that you can feel and touch, and that you've probably had to learn about in school to pass biology exams at some point. However, unless you've continued your personal education in spiritual and holistic circles, you may have missed out on the information that you also have various energetic systems that operate through and beyond the physical body.

You may have come across terms like the 'emotional body', the 'mental body', the 'aura', and the 'chakra system'. These are metaphysical energy systems, some of which certain people can see, and which can be detected through various scientific instruments. These energetic bodies hold all the information and wisdom of who (and what) you truly are – beyond just the thoughts you think, the emotions you feel, and the tissues and organs your doctor can describe to you.

Your energetic bodies interact with other people's energetic bodies and, through such interaction, you transfer information simply by being in proximity to someone. Within your energetic systems you have energy centers, known as chakras. There are seven main chakras situated in the body, ranging from the root chakra, which is located in the perineum, to the crown chakra, which is found on top of the head. A chakra is an energy center in the body that draws in energy from the surroundings. It also gives out energy from your body into the environment, too. This energetic exchange is rich in information about both your internal and external environments.

Each energy center is related to a specific aspect of our lives. Here, we are particularly curious about the third chakra, situated at the solar plexus. This is the one that governs self-esteem and our sense of identity. This is the one we are going to use to unleash our Money Mojo.

If you already do energy work, you will probably be aware that traditionally the second chakra (located just below the belly button) is thought to be the one that relates to material issues and finance. However, from working specifically with people who want more money in their lives, I've found that if the third chakra isn't functioning properly, working on the second chakra is ineffective. Once the third chakra is operating properly, individuals develop rock-solid self-esteem and believe they deserve more wealth.

I know this seems back to front, but just try it on for size. Anyone who studies chakra balancing generally advocates starting with the lower chakras and working their way upward. But we're starting at the third chakra because we're going to wire ourselves for wealth as efficiently as possible, and I've found that this just works. Why? In essence, when this third energy center is depleted we find ourselves in sabotage mode, constantly operating to slow things down and letting opportunities pass us by because subconsciously we feel we're not ready to experience the next level of success – even if consciously we're doing everything we know to get it to work. Correcting the imbalance in the third chakra goes a long way toward increasing self-esteem and the amount of responsibility (and income) a person feels able to take on.

This was certainly the case with Joanne who, by her own admission, felt she was not ready for massive success. A very competent marketing consultant, she knew exactly what she should do in order to promote her business and generate more income. And she did the first stages of this process quite happily. In fact, she would go round doing lots of presentations and networking, meeting lots of people, and building up a fantastic following and database. Yet it all seemed to fall apart when it came to converting this activity into cash.

As it transpired, she was afraid to take on more paying clients because she wasn't sure she had what it took to deliver outstanding value. As such, she concentrated her activity on building her list, so that when she felt ready she would be able to deliver the kind of value people could pay for. But in the meantime she was resistant to taking even enough money to cover her expenses. She also knew all the techniques for converting this value into money: she had loads of ideas for products and training packages she could offer, but rather than do this, she would allow herself to get distracted and do everything but take on clients.

Of course, this wasn't immediately evident. On the surface her big problem (and what she herself would say), was that she was always too busy to do anything that would bring in money! In other words, she was too busy being busy. But this happens so often. We get distracted. Or more accurately, we distract ourselves from the task that will make the difference. We scatter our energy and focus, so that we don't make too much progress in one direction. Sometimes it's because we're not ready to deliver what we promise; sometimes we aren't ready to accept money for something other than a paid job delivering someone else's product. Sometimes we just don't like receiving money from clients directly. Do you know anyone who does this? Perhaps that person is very close to you? Perhaps that person is reading these pages right now!

Now, you've probably already found that getting results is a great way to build your confidence and self-esteem. What often happens, though, is you start to get results and then something happens to take everything off the boil. When good things start to happen, we get excited and start dreaming. We are thrilled that our plans are all about to come together. But at the same time, we are scared witless at the prospect of actually getting what we want. No one likes to admit it, but success is scary. And big success is massively scary.

So what happens is that we freeze up energetically. We get a tightening in our chest. Our mind starts racing ten to the dozen about all the things that could go wrong and all the reasons we're not yet ready, and starts projecting forward all the possible obstacles we are going to have to contend with if we are to be successful. The Universe will then respond to our feeling that we're not ready yet by withdrawing the opportunity until we *are* ready.

Our internal struggle is relayed in our energy field like a massive beacon, ready for anyone to pick up on as soon as we start talking about the latest opportunity or success. People know when we don't think we really deserve it.

But that's not to say that we should put off doing things until we feel sure we're ready. Quite the opposite. In fact, it's the biggest, scariest goals that are most worthy of our efforts, simply because they will have the most effect on our positive development. So, don't shrink from the opportunity that scares you, but instead try to let go of all the 'I can't' energy around it, which is deeply layered in the psyche and energy systems we've just been talking about. Take on the tasks that make you excited and terrified at the same time, because you get an amazing opportunity to release all the negativity that's holding you back. You then naturally achieve the goal, as if it were just a walk in the park.

We can increase our self-esteem, then, by dumping all our pent-up emotional baggage. By contrast, if we stay in our comfort zone, we never bring it to the surface to process it. The other great thing about this concept is that as soon as you start getting rid of the baggage, your whole world of possibilities expands. Remember in the introduction where we talked about how when one area of your life expands, all other areas do as well? The same goes here. Making a breakthrough with emotional baggage related to one particular area of your life increases the boundary of your comfort zone massively in all directions.

I experienced this myself before selling one of my first courses. I had a crisis of confidence when my third chakra was releasing all the 'garbage' necessary to free me up to achieve the sales goal I had set myself. As a result I was able to let go of a whole load of insecurities that I hadn't even been previously aware I was harboring. These included asking myself who I thought I was, delivering such a course, wondering if I had enough qualifications, and querying if I could help make a difference in people's lives.

When I tell people about my doubts they laugh in disbelief, but how we appear outwardly is not a true reflection of what is going on internally. By the same token, as you will discover when we talk about emotions our internal state is constantly changing, and it's okay to feel insecure at times, as long as we allow this sensation to pass through. It's good to allow emotions to come up and to leave, as then we're not wasting massive amounts of energy suppressing them.

So what happened after my third chakra had finished releasing my insecurities? I felt much better, and happier. I ran the webinar, had a great time, and shared loads of useful insights with the people on the line. Places on the webinar sold incredibly well, and I then went on to run a really successful and enjoyable course, and many more after that. The participants received excellent value. In fact, some of the individuals on that course are still coaching clients today and continue to go from strength to strength, using the very techniques we're unfolding here. In summary, I ditched all the baggage associated with that one issue, my comfort zone increased massively, and I've never had that same stuck feeling associated with running courses since.

But what if I hadn't let go of all the mind stuff and emotional garbage saying that I wasn't good enough, wasn't qualified enough, wasn't prepared enough? The Universe would have picked up on this resonance pattern and said, 'You're not ready? Then I'm going to keep you safe and not let you make a fool of yourself by giving you the opportunity to step up and prove yourself. I'm not going to let anyone come on your course.' Best to ditch the doubt and baggage, isn't it?

So, let's concentrate on you now. Where in your life or business are you hanging back from doing something under the pretense of being too busy, not having the resources, or not knowing what to do or how to do it? What are your doubts? What baggage would you like to get rid of?

Write down one or two things that spring to mind, right now:

1. _Don't have enough money_

2. _Don't know what to do_

The next thing to realize is that it's okay to be hanging back, that it's okay to be stuck for a while. Now you've identified where there's a blockage you can remove it – and once you do so, you can excel. Log this, because we'll be coming back to unblock it in the next chapter.

So, if we accept that self-esteem is a prerequisite for attracting wealth and holding onto it, the other side of the same coin is something we also need to consider before we move on. And what is the other side of self-esteem? It's self-responsibility.

Taking Responsibility for Yourself

That's right – self-responsibility and self-esteem are two sides of the same coin. Energetically they hit the same frequency when you're working on the issue in terms of body work and energy patterns. They have the same 'feel' to them. They also both operate out of the third chakra, as they are third-chakra issues.

This means that as we increase our self-esteem, we are able to take more responsibility for our lives, our situations, our thoughts, feelings and behaviours. Without self-esteem, it is very easy for us as individuals to say that our state of wealth, or health 'is not our fault.'

Think back to when you've felt helpless and not responsible for things in your environment. How much self-worth did you truly have? Were you blaming something, or someone else, to protect yourself from feeling worthless? It's an emotionally mature individual who can hold up their hands and take responsibility for every area of their lives, without falling into self-pity or feeling like a victim.

You see, true self-responsibility is about knowing that everything is within your control, and no one is to blame. Let me explain. Often when I start coaching someone who hasn't already come across this idea, they will say that their finances are in such a poor state because they don't get paid enough, or they have too many bills to pay, or the cost of living is too high, or someone else owes them money, and so on. But if we buy into this illusion, we are saying that we are completely at the mercy of external events and we negate what we are creating and manifesting in the world around us.

By contract, if we can 'man up' and take responsibility for whatever fiscal carnage or affluent delight we find ourselves in, we are back in control and can operate at a high enough energetic level to affect what happens next.

What's more, even if we are in a financial mess, if we take responsibility for it, we immediately cease hemorrhaging energy out of the third chakra, and instead encourage it to start nourishing our self-esteem. (You'll notice a massive increase in the energy available to you the *moment* you make this decision.)

So, this being the case, the first step in nurturing your ever-so-important self-esteem, and therefore your Money Mojo, is to take back responsibility for *whatever* is going on in your life. If your job is uninspiring, take back responsibility as the person who took the job in the first place. Take responsibility as the person who has turned up to that same job every day since then. Take back the responsibility for that bad back, or that ongoing illness or allergy. Take back responsibility for feeling fed up or depressed because you hate your financial situation or you haven't worked out yet how to make more money. Take back responsibility for eating too much and exercising too little. Take back responsibility for the way the people around you treat you – whether it's well or badly.

By doing this we are then able to accept that we created these circumstances and are responsible – but not to blame. This, in turn, gives us the power to change the situation. (Incidentally, blame is disempowering and is a lower energy. It doesn't help to fix the problem, so it's simply not useful. Besides, you deserve better than blame. You deserve love and understanding from your inner Self in order to put the situation on a footing you're happier with.)

Once you have taken responsibility for your situation, you are then in a position to do something about it. Taking responsibility puts you back in the driving seat, back in control. This is incredibly liberating and a refreshing place to be. Often people making this shift in their perception will feel like a big heavy weight has suddenly been lifted from their shoulders. This is because they have started to pull back the energy that they were allowing to drain out of their system.

Take Robert, who was in a job he hated. He would complain about it, but then each time he would start to re-wind and end his rant by saying 'It's not that bad, it's getting better.' It wasn't getting better, though. Sometimes his situation seemed to improve, depending on the coaching work he'd done with me, but as he avoided doing the work he needed to do in order to dump the emotional baggage, real progress was slow. Robert's boss was habitually rude to him and demanding, but didn't treat his co-workers in the same way. His girlfriend was needy and would make unrealistic demands on him. He also had a friend who would rope him into one hare-brained scheme after another. He was being pushed from pillar to post and allowing others to use him whenever they pleased. But this was all a result of what he was giving out through his energy field: his whole aura was self-deprecating. He was ready to accept maltreatment to avoid any form of confrontation.

Telling himself it wasn't that bad was a compromise he made with himself every time he went to work at that job that he hated. To maintain the status quo and keep him in that job, his mind would constantly tell him things like: 'Just one more month and you can complete the project and find something else to do.' 'You're coping better these days,' or 'Okay, so you were frustrated today, but tomorrow will be easier as you'll be left alone for most of the time.'

One day, Robert decided to take back his power. Having done some serious work on his third chakra and on building his self-esteem, he had enough confidence to end the disempowering relationship with his girlfriend. As he worked on his self-esteem, using the exercise at the end of this chapter and the technique in the next chapter, he was able to turn things around at work very quickly. The relationship with his boss mellowed and relaxed. The project progressed more easily with less drama and struggle. Even the friend who had constantly tried to manipulate him seemed to fade into the background.

Robert's energy levels went up when he decided to take back responsibility for himself, his thoughts and opinions, and what he should be doing with his time every moment of the day. He made the decision to reclaim his power from the people he had attracted into his life to teach him that very lesson.

You Create Your Reality with the Thoughts You Think

If it's true you create your reality with the thoughts you think, why would you consciously create a situation that is making you stressed and miserable? It's absurd, right? Yes, consciously, if you had a choice between having many times more money in your bank account or having less, you would naturally choose more. But the reality you are experiencing right now is the result of the thoughts you've been thinking in the moments leading up till now.

You see, your brain emits energy and information. You'll probably have seen pictures of the brain taken with devices that measure electromagnetic emissions. Your brain sits in a sea or a field of awareness – a field of information, if you prefer. This is how it connects up with everything that exists, including the 'collective unconscious', the Jungian concept of universal consciousness that we are all part of. It is the brain, acting as a transmitter and receiver, that allows our thoughts to hook up to what is going on in the 'web' of consciousness. In spiritual circles this feeling is referred to as 'oneness.'

So, here is your brain, sitting in the field, communicating with other brains on a subconscious level, whilst the busy cerebral cortex is more concerned with catching that train, or what you should have for lunch. Every thought the brain thinks, however, is broadcast into this common field of awareness. And the very act of having that thought attracts similar ones back to it. This is why holding an intention, or a picture of how you choose something to manifest, is so incredibly powerful. You can literally pull that event into your reality just by thinking about it.

Now, thoughts that are going ten to the dozen get diluted. But if you stop and consider for a moment, you will notice that most of the thoughts you think are repeats of previous thoughts. You will find you run certain thought patterns again and again and again. So, say you are constantly worried about missing your train, by rehearsing this scenario in your brain and sending it out into the sea of awareness, you are resonating constantly in the energy pattern of missing your train. And guess what happens... Right! You miss the train.

Now that you know this, all you have to do is decide that you are always ahead of time and you will always catch your train easily. You just hold a picture of yourself catching your train in your mind. And if you can keep this as a more dominant thought than the previous one of missing the train, you can trust that the more favorable outcome will prevail.

The same goes for making money. If you hold thoughts of having enough, and having the freedom and cash to do whatever you choose, this will be the reality you attract into your world.

And it all starts with cultivating a good, solid sense of self-esteem, so that when you choose these thoughts, they prevail easily over any doubts or fleeting feelings of unworthiness.

The Self-Esteem Map

Here's a great exercise for increasing your self-esteem. It lays the foundation for the work we're going to do later in the book, so it's worth taking the time to do it now.

This was the first exercise I did when I realized that self-esteem was such a fundamental key to success. Believe it or not, it doesn't matter how educated or skilled you are, or what you physically do in your day-to-day activities. But if you can approach every activity with high self-esteem, it's almost as if you end up playing a different game – one that's easier, more fun, and one you're more likely to succeed at. I noticed a huge difference in my ability to get projects off the ground after I had spent a few days working on this exercise.

The first thing to do is to recognize what it is that you want to achieve and bolster your confidence in. It might be that you want to attract more customers, or get your marketing straight, or sort out the way you deliver your product. Whatever it is, make sure it is within your circle of influence for this exercise, and then take out a large sheet of paper and pop those summary words in a circle in the middle of the page.

We're going to create a bubble diagram, but this is a bubble diagram with a twist. Normally bubble diagrams are used to unlock all the creative ideas we have around a particular subject. What we're going to do here though, is to use it to come up with all the thoughts we have buried in our minds that could possibly support us. We're basically looking to create a map of all the reasons (big and small) why we deserve to have that outcome, and why we are capable of achieving it. This is a Self-Esteem Map.

So, for instance, if you don't have enough clients for whatever reason and you'd like to have more, you'd put the words 'more clients' in the central bubble. You'd then draw other bubbles stemming out from the central bubble, on the end of spokes, and write in them the reasons why you are capable of having more clients, and why you deserve to have more clients. For example, you could put that you're excellent at what you do, that you have trained with such and such a person, that you have x-y-z qualifications, and so on.

The brain finds this format easy to understand as you're working with associations, so once you get going you'll find it easy to come up with reasons.

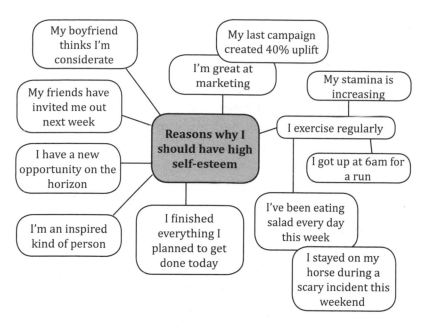

Figure 2.1: Example of a Self-Esteem Map

Now, this isn't like goal setting, so don't get hung up about it. We're just looking to counteract the effects of the ego and mind chatter, which are constantly putting us down, so we can do the rest of this work in a positive frame of mind. You're going to be like a honed athlete when it comes to making magic in your projects and your finances! A professional athlete won't tolerate negative people around them, particularly just before they perform. This kind of negativity can make them weak. Their coaches are constantly telling them they have worked hard and they will win. They program themselves to give 110 per cent and then give even more because they know they deserve this victory.

By making your own Self-Esteem Map, you'll be doing the same thing for yourself – ousting the negative chatter of the ego. You're not just looking to fill the page, you're looking to come up with around 200 reasons. 'Two hundred? You're kidding me!' I hear you shout. Believe me; if you want this to work, and you want to make a positive impact on your finances, you need to get to at least 200. Any less than this I've found just isn't enough.

Now you may think that this is going to take absolutely ages, but I assure you it won't! Not once you get going. And you can keep coming back to it between other tasks, because as you turn it over in your mind, new streams of thought will come to you. Remember, we're digging deep into the psyche to lay some positive roots – it can't be done over the surface in a few seconds, or it won't last.

Take your time. You'll be glad you did. You probably have a particular area of your business or yourself that you'd like to work on to increase your confidence in that area. So it's okay to get specific around a particular issue. Just pop that issue down in the central bubble and find reasons to support it in the bubbles that spring from that central idea.

Some people find they would benefit from some extra self-esteem around charging their clients more (particularly if they are in a service-based business). Sometimes individuals feel they lack the ability to stand on stage and speak about their work. Sometimes people need more confidence in communicating with their potential customers, or even in just allowing people to give them money in exchange for their services. For example, let's consider the issue of accepting money for your services.

Depending on where you are on your journey of Money-Mojo mastery, you may already find this easy, or you may find it is the one thing that is holding you back. Wherever you are, think of it at your level and come up with 200 plus reasons why you deserve to have people give you money in exchange for the service you provide for them.

The beauty of doing this in a bubble diagram is that it allows you to think freely. You may associate some things with certain other reasons you come up with. Trying to do this in a linear list is more restrictive. In this exercise you can work back and forth and around the issue in the central bubble. Keep going. The idea is to build a solid foundation, in much the same way as you form a belief.

Once you have around 200 reasons as to why you deserve to be well rewarded for the work you do for your clients, you will have less resistance to having the cash come in, having people pay their bills, or setting your rates at the appropriate level.

If you get to the point where you're struggling to think of more things to write down, keep pushing, because that will be where the gems are. Don't be precious about what you write down and what you don't write down. You don't have to keep your ideas to general categories or abstract items. For example, if you've written down that you've had satisfied clients, and then later you think of one or two in particular for whom you did a really good job, then write them down separately. Give yourself full credit for everything.

And remember, we're not looking to log massive victories over other people. Self-esteem is an inside job. It begins and ends with ourselves, so if you felt good about making some positive changes to a single page on your website, then stick that down. It all adds up.

Make a decision to be courageous, and do it in spite of feeling afraid or unsure it will produce the outcome. By actually taking action and doing this exercise you will start to feel more in control. Once you're rolling you have overcome the initial fear and inertia, and if the action you're taking isn't working, all you need to do is make a few minor adjustments. This is much easier than trying to get going in the first place, because you've already made a decision to produce a result – and that result may not necessarily change the world, but again, it will contribute to your self-esteem and make you realize that you are a 'can-do' person.

You are worthy of being wealthy, and having more than enough money, love, and good health throughout a long and prosperous lifetime. You just have to choose to allow it to manifest as your immediate reality.

Points to Remember

- Self-esteem can be cultivated

- Self-esteem is essential to being able to make and keep money

- Self-esteem makes manifestation a thousand times easier and more effective

- Self-esteem and self-responsibility go hand in hand

Next up – the second key to wiring yourself for wealth.

Chapter 3
Key 2: Dump the Emotional Baggage

Now that we have looked at ways to increase our self-esteem, it's time to consider the next key, which is how to rid ourselves of the emotional baggage that is preventing us from attaining the wealth we desire.

We all have talents, but sometimes we are unable to develop them to the full because there is something holding us back. For example, suppose that you're naturally suited to presenting from the stage yet have a fear of public speaking. Or what if you excel at selling an idea to people, but have a thing against sales? What if you're a natural negotiator, but have a block around making money? Or what if you think that doing deals always means someone wins and someone loses?

So let's now consider how we can remove the obstacles that cause us to hang back and not do what we know we *should* be doing. The first thing we need to learn is how to release the emotions that are creating the obstacles, so that we can then take *effective* action concerning more practical and strategic matters.

In the last chapter we discovered that having high self-esteem was essential to being able to have, and to hold on to, money. We also alluded to the fact that low self-esteem is merely a symptom of having our spirit and thought processes crushed by excess emotional baggage. To increase our self-esteem effectively (key 1), we need to let go of this heavy, disempowering emotional baggage (key 2). I will be showing you a few simple processes for how to do this later in the chapter.

On a purely energetic level our emotions around money and self-worth determine the amount of cash we allow into our lives. At a more basic level, whether we realize it or not, all our decisions are emotional. For example, whether we buy something or not is essentially an emotional decision – we simply justify it with logic after we've already made the decision. Whether or not we take on a particular belief is also an emotional decision. When we choose a job, or accept a client, it's an emotional decision. If we are generally living in an attitude of fear and lack, we are likely to compromise what we truly want because we worry that if we don't, we won't have money or security, or another opportunity to create these things. This is why we sometimes accept tasks or clients without first contemplating whether we are best served by doing so. And negotiating our pay or prices is also an emotional event. How many times do you drop your rates or reduce your asking price, just because you are fearful people won't give you the contract or buy your product?

Can you see how our emotions set the thermostat for our levels of wealth? Dropping our emotional baggage is therefore essential if we are going to allow ourselves to have more money.

Now, most of us would rather pack our emotions into suitcases, store them away in a deep dark closet in our minds, and throw away the key. But like a clothes hoarder's ever-expanding wardrobe, this only aids the accumulation of more baggage and junk. Emotions are not meant to be stacked away in a closet, *they are meant to be felt.* Often we shy away from this. We try to outrun them. We eat. We drink alcohol. We drink coffee. We take in excessive amounts of sugar. Some of us take other forms of drugs. We do anything to *avoid having to feel.* We numb ourselves daily in subconscious attempts not to have to feel the emotions that we are generating. And in doing this we distract ourselves from the subconscious programming we set up in our neurology, which dictates how much money we let ourselves have.

How Does This Relate to Our Money Mojo?

The emotions we resist feeling are the very guidance system we have been born with. When used and processed correctly, our emotions will tell us if we are on or off course. So they are there as indicators. When we feel sad, or depressed, it's our body's way of showing us we are living out of harmony with ourselves. For example, guilt is a way of showing us that we are acting out of integrity with our spirit. Anger is a signal that we have allowed someone to violate our spirit in some way. By contrast, joy and peace are ways of telling us we are on track and in alignment with ourselves.

It's okay to feel emotions – in fact, they are an essential guidance system. And yet we live in a society where emotions are frowned upon. We're told it's not acceptable to be confused, or angry, or sad, and so on. Yet it is regarded as okay to be 'medically depressed', 'stressed', or 'tired' – these seem to be socially acceptable states to be in.

We particularly have it upside down when it comes to confusion – and this is an important thing to remember as we rewire ourselves for wealth – because we often get confused while we're in the state of flux between clinging to old money beliefs and adopting new ones. And people generally don't like being confused. In fact, most of us find it scary, as somewhere deep in our psyche our ego has convinced us that if we are confused, and we don't know what is going on, we aren't safe. So we have taken on the belief that if we are confused, our survival is threatened. No wonder we spend so much time trying to figure everything out. And no wonder that once we think we have it figured out, we resist anything that challenges that picture. But, in reality, this is just another decision we make based on the emotional sensation of feeling confused.

It is worth noting, before you start working on releasing your emotional baggage, that in live coaching sessions I've found confusion is actually *an incredibly productive and useful state* to be in. It is exciting when this state kicks in because it's a sign that the brain is re-jigging itself. It's letting go of all the old, counter-productive thoughts and beliefs, and allowing new ones to take shape. It's when the old synaptic connections (which are the physical hardware of our beliefs and thought processes) die out and let new ones take their place. And because we have let go of a heap of emotional baggage, we begin to operate at a higher energetic frequency, resulting in the new connections that are being built at a higher frequency, too. In this way, the new brain we are forming is wired at a higher energy level and so becomes capable of higher-level processing.

So you see it *is* okay to be confused. And it's also okay to feel emotions, because then we can process them. When we allow ourselves to experience feelings, we enable our emotional system to process the events related to those sensations. Once we process them, we take on the emotional experience as new wisdom, which becomes absorbed into our energy system as energetic information. In this way, emotional experiences are like taking in food.

Say an event happens, and we experience it emotionally. We take it in like food or information. Next we chew on the new information, seeing how it integrates with our current system of beliefs. Then we swallow and accept it into our system, and allow ourselves to process it. Somewhere along the line it gets absorbed into our system in a useful way to nourish us, and to add to our growth and evolution.

However, if we don't allow ourselves to chew on an event and process it properly, it is likely to cause a blockage. We suppress it so that we don't feel the emotion, and we just put it away in a box where it festers and prevents us from processing and metabolizing it, and allowing it to contribute to our growth.

To summarize, if we're not processing and releasing the emotions we experience, we are suppressing them. If we're suppressing them, we're holding on to unnecessary emotional baggage.

In a moment, we will be learning exactly how to let go of this unwanted baggage and how to stop ourselves suppressing our feelings.

What You Think Matters

Our emotions and the way we feel help to direct the ever-changing energetic field of the world around us, which in turn dictates what happens in the material world. And this means that our emotions affect whether or not we can manifest more money.

By letting go of the emotional baggage that we have accumulated, we free our energy system up to create things the way we want them, without the doubts and negative thinking that create the opposite of what we desire.

Traditional thinking holds that the world and the matter in it are solid, dense, and unchanging. But as we release more of our emotional baggage, we tend to become aware of a new 'reality' emerging around us – one in which everything is dynamic and ever-changing. 'Normal', 'logical' thinking suggests that this must be a figment of our imagination or a misinterpretation of our senses. Yet in our new reality thoughts can become matter by manifesting and we realize that what we thought of as 'real' is no more dense and solid than a dream.

When we shift to this world view we can more readily accept that every thought we think is creating our world. This means that we are in fact determining what is going on in our lives and we're not at the mercy of events. We are creating all the time, whether we like the result or not.

Everything that we are experiencing in our existence right now is the direct result of the thoughts we were thinking at some point before now. Every thought we think at this moment will in some way manifest in the future.

But how can we change this underlying, deep-rooted, and mostly subconscious belief that the world is solid? Our very lives are built on this foundation. Through releasing our emotional baggage, we gain the opportunity to drop all the redundant thoughts and beliefs that hold us back from understanding how the world truly operates. By releasing the emotions, thoughts, and feelings around our current reality, we are able to take the brake off our ability to manifest, so that by merely holding an intention it will come into being.

The crucial thing to realize when we find ourselves dissatisfied with the way things are in any aspect of our lives, is that we have created it that way because of the stuff we are holding on to, which causes us to think the thoughts we habitually have. This then creates it physically. The longer we hold on to bad feelings, the heavier they become, and the stronger the resonance pattern they set up. By releasing these negative patterns at the emotional level, we are able to disrupt them in the emotional, mental, and physical bodies and free ourselves of the behavioral patterns that produce the physical manifestations in our environment. In other words, when we are stuck, the place to start overcoming the 'stuckness' is within our own emotional system.

Now here's just a note before we dive into releasing this emotional baggage. I want you to know that baggage of any description isn't a 'bad' thing. It's not something to push against or to reject. It's nothing to be ashamed of. It just *is*. It's just a natural result of living, making mistakes, getting things right, and working through consequences. There is no good or bad in the bigger picture of life.

If we had a choice between having an easy and effortless life or one that is hard work and a struggle, the smart people amongst us would choose the easy and effortless option. However, this emotional stuff we gather is only called emotional 'baggage' because we hang on to it and carry it around with us. If we were to just let things go, as and when they happen, we would stay fully present and poised in the moment, and free of such baggage.

Sometimes, our emotional baggage becomes buried so deeply that we forget it's there. We may not be able to recall anything traumatic that has happened, but the truth is that all the time we interact with people, things happen, and we make decisions based on how those things make us feel. In some ways, the baggage that we are talking about is just the sum of lots of decisions that don't serve us, which we've made in those fleeting moments.

An example could be something as simple as someone disapproving of us because we were a little too loud at the dinner table (and I'm not just talking about when we were children). On feeling this disapproval, we might choose to feel hurt, or to protect ourselves by putting up a barrier by saying to ourselves that this person's opinion doesn't matter. And/or we could justify our own actions by saying that everyone else was talking loudly, too, or that we just got overexcited.

No matter how we deal with the resulting emotions, we're still trying to *manage* the feeling, which takes a huge effort. Often, we'll put it into a little box and label the incident in one of the ways we've just described, just so that we can cope with it in our mind. This may work short-term – but over long periods of time 'managing' our thoughts and emotions clogs us up and exhausts us. The more energy-efficient thing to do would be *not* to manage the emotion, but to allow it to pass through our body and let it go.

So now that you know that letting go is an option, let's talk about how to release your emotions, rather than hanging on to them.

Releasing the Sensation

Think of something right now that bothers you. It might be a person, an incident, or a situation you're currently facing. Notice your body and your breathing. See if there is a heaviness in your body anywhere – you'll probably feel it somewhere in your stomach, chest, throat, or even in your head. If right now your awareness is absorbed in what you are reading, you may need to take it out of your head down and into your abdomen, or even further to the base of your spine if you're quite cerebral and analytical. From here, can you notice any particular sensations? Is there a heaviness anywhere?

If the answer is yes, then great – you're already aware of your body. If no, there is a chance you have shut down your awareness so that you don't notice the energies present in your body. The good news is that it is fairly easy to tune into them again. It just takes a bit of practice and an intention to notice how you're feeling and where. You can practice by homing in on your emotions and the sensations in your body in your day-to-day activities. You'll soon tune in.

Assuming you can feel something, just allow that feeling to be there. This is the first step in releasing – becoming aware of the blockage or heaviness you are about to let go. The next step is to make the decision to let it go. Your intention should be powerful enough to allow this to happen without you having to do anything. In this situation I sometimes find it useful to first ask myself the following three questions:

1. Is there the possibility that I could let it go?

Intellectually you know there is. You've let things go in the past. There have been lots of things that have happened to you, or upset you, and now you can't even remember them, so you have probably just released them.

2. If you could, would you?

Sometimes people answer emphatically 'Yes' at this point. If this is your response, great! You've already embraced the essence of letting go and will find it very easy to make progress.

Occasionally, though, this needs a little more discussion, because sometimes people choose to hold on to the cause of their blockage. Perhaps they aren't ready to release it yet – in which case, that's okay. But what I've found is that people tend to get bored of hanging on to a feeling that naturally wants to leave – so generally it just disappears anyway. Besides, it can be uncomfortable to have a heavy sensation sitting on your chest, so why would you want to hang on to it?

We are not releasing our feelings to let someone else off the hook, for example by letting go of resentment toward them for something they did to us. Letting go doesn't change what they did. But it does change the way we feel about it. So instead of feeling angry, hurt, and negative about an experience, we can let ourselves out of prison and stop our own torture by choosing to let go of the hurt and feel better. Remember that old adage about resentment being a poison you drink expecting the other person to die?

Sometimes there is a need to explain why whatever happened is so bad that you don't feel you should let it go. That's fine, too. If you can relate to this, feel free to write down anything you want to express and get it off your chest. You can then go back and see if you would now say yes to the above question: 'If you could, would you?'

The next thing to remember here is that it is *your* decision. You can either hang on to the feelings that are uncomfortable and ultimately zapping your energy, or you can choose to let them go and feel good. It's a choice. And you're a smart person.

3. When would be a good time to let this feeling go?

This is entirely up to you, but the way to make the most rapid progress is to answer 'Now!' This gives you the permission you need to let it go. Try it for yourself. Yes, now! Put the book down for a few moments and take this opportunity right now. Go ahead – work through the three questions, holding in your mind something that is bothering you right now.

1. Is there the possibility you could let it go?

2. If you could, would you?

3. When is a good time?

The more you can do this the lighter you will feel. Keep going, it takes practice!

The trick is *not* to try and control the feeling. Be open to experiencing it, and then allow it to evaporate. That way, you've fully owned and experienced that emotion and you don't need to keep recreating circumstances to feel that way.

This is how we release an emotion – by feeling it as physical sensation and then letting it go.

Letting Go of Thoughts

Let's now explore how to let go of a thought. The thing about thoughts is that they are overrated! Getting into and staying in a state of Flow is less about *thinking* and more about *being*. If we're thinking, we're not being; if we're thinking, we're not living in the moment.

Another problem with thoughts is that we have too many of them. They are fleeting. And then one thought leads to another – and another and another. Most of the time, unless we're present in the moment, our thoughts tend to be on a loop. Apparently, we have something like 50,000 thoughts a day – but a huge percentage of those are repeats of previous ones. In essence we actually rehearse thought processes. And generally this is not a helpful thing.

Thoughts in our brains start off as mere chemical tracks that get fired again and again, but the more we practice them, the more physical and material they become. Eventually these thoughts thicken and develop the neurons they run along, making the thought process more and more automatic. Practice, does indeed make perfect – even when you don't want it to.

So, what emotional releasing allows us to do is to drop the thoughts so that we can be present in the moment, because this is where our power lies. You see, when we're in the moment, our mind stops whirring and becomes still. And at this point we can connect up to our higher selves and allow ourselves to be guided.

In most of our waking time, we are aware of ourselves as separate individuals. We appear to have a mind and a body and we seem separate from other people. However, when we drop thoughts of limitation (the thoughts that keep us believing this), what we actually discover is that our consciousness is connected up to everyone else's, which in turn is part of the oneness that makes up everything that exists. We realize that this idea – that we are separate entities with our own thoughts, feelings, problems, and beliefs – is in fact an illusion that we've put in place in order to experience what it feels like to be limited.

The whole quest for enlightenment is a journey to realize that our separateness is a falsehood and that, in truth, we are everyone around us, and all that is. I like to use the analogy of a comb that has individual teeth. At their furthest points, the teeth of a comb appear to be separate pieces of plastic. However, when we look at the bigger picture (the whole comb), we realize that each tooth is connected up along the spine.

It's similar with human beings – we are connected by the collective consciousness. This also explains how individuals can discover the same thing at the same time at several points on the globe. For instance, Leibniz and Newton both developed calculus at the same time; Charles Darwin and Alfred Russell Wallace both constructed their Theories of Evolution simultaneously. Each was plugged into the collective consciousness, and it is almost as if it was the designated time for these ideas to be brought into the general consciousness of the world.

Now, imagine how creative and insightful you could become if you spent less time running those rehearsed thoughts over and over and more time allowing fresh guidance to come into your awareness through having a quiet and still mind. What difference might you see in your own life – in your projects, your finances, and in your interactions with others if you could grasp that everything in existence was part of one and the same. Would you be less fearful? Would you be more caring and understanding? Would you be more intuitive in your decision-making?

So, how do you achieve a quiet mind? The rest of this book is going to walk you through just that. Through the strategies of dropping your emotional baggage and negative thoughts, and the discovery that you are *not* the mind, but you have complete control over it, you will learn how to make it still, and how to open up your awareness to our interconnectedness. If you use these techniques you will discover a deep trust in the Universe and a connection to your own higher self. You will cultivate an ability to surrender to what is, and to be able to accept anything you don't like in your world, which will then give you the power to change rather than resist it. You will have the ultimate control over designing and shaping your own world, and making it exactly as you wish it to be. And that includes your money situation!

Now, let's return to the topic of how to drop unhelpful thoughts. Letting go of such thoughts allows old thought patterns and emotions to resurface. When this happens you are able to release them, too, making you feel lighter and freer. Once you start redirecting your thoughts, the neural pathways that were previously used frequently by your limiting thoughts, disintegrate and change. You can physically reverse the effects these old thoughts had on your brain.

Thoughts move too quickly for us, as beginners, to catch every one of them. After you've been letting go of them for a while, you'll begin to notice that they slow down and you'll be able to release them much more easily. But one of the things that can really help us whilst we're learning to let go is the fact that thoughts and emotions are interlinked: one creates the other. So, in fact, if we release an emotion, we can also release the overriding thoughts associated with that emotion. But as we let go of the thoughts, we can also let go of the underlying emotion. It's so productive!

Often when people are new to releasing, and they start letting go of emotions, they can be suddenly swamped with distracting thoughts. If this happens, all we do is let go of the thoughts that arise, as and when they come up.

Conversely, we may also be releasing thoughts and then get swamped with emotions. In either scenario, the thing to do is to just keep letting go of both.

As we've already said, there are some tricky things about thoughts. They can be sticky, particularly when they are caught up with emotions. As such, it is more difficult for us to just let them go. What we need is a technique for categorizing them, and thus distancing ourselves from them, so we find it easier to let them go. So, here we go. This technique also simplifies the letting-go process. All thoughts, emotions or reactions on our part can be seen as one of three basic categories of 'want.'

1. Wanting love, praise, recognition, or approval; or lacking acceptance of something

2. Wanting to control, change, or direct something

3. Wanting security, safety, to avoid fear or dying

By seeing each emotion, thought, or sensation as one of these basic three wants we are able to distance ourselves from the emotion, or the validity of the thought, and then just let it go. Notice, we never question whether that thought is true. We don't need to engage with it. We simply let it go.

Here's an overview of how the sequence goes. We'll come back to talking about the *wanting love, wanting to change something,* and *wanting security* categories shortly. Now:

• Think of the thought that troubles you.

- Can you categorize it as either wanting love, wanting to change something, or wanting security? (You will get a sense that it is one, or any combination of the three.)

- Whichever want it is, could you let it go?

- If you could, would you?

- When is a good time?

Do you see how we've built on what we did before? Try it with another problem now, and just notice how you feel freer each time you let go.

Wanting versus Having

So why are we letting go of wanting these things? Surely it is nice to be in control, to have other peoples' love, praise, and recognition, and security?

Yes, it is absolutely. Except *wanting* and *having* are two very different things. In fact, as I am about to show you, energetically it is the *wanting* that is preventing you from *having*.

Think of something you really want. Is it a shiny new car? Or perhaps it's an exotic vacation? Or could it be the beautiful dress you saw in an exclusive store the other week? How does that *feel*?

Now think of something you already have. This could be your home, the car you drive, the computer you work at, the cup of coffee sitting by you right now, and so on. Now, how does *that* feel?

You will probably notice that the thing you want and the thing you already have evoke different emotions in you and have a different energetic feel to them, too. You probably have no attachment to the thing you have, but a far more exciting pull toward the thing you want.

Now you may be amazed to learn that it is this same pull or wanting that is *stopping* you from having what you want. Rather than a *pull*, it is an energetic *push* or barrier keeping the item just out of reach. Thus wanting and having are mutually exclusive – you can't want and have at the same time.

This is my definition of 'wanting', taken from my *Emotional Releasing 101* course:

- to be lacking or deficient
- to feel the absence of
- to be destitute
- to fall short by
- a lack, an absence, or a craving.

So whilst we are resonating at the frequency of lack and being without, we are energetically at the opposite of the frequency of having. The world around us then allows that to be so. Until we let go of the lack, we can never operate energetically as having, and thus this will never become our experience in the external world.

We want so many things. It's almost a habit. But it's a habit we can use to get rid of all the underlying emotional stuff. Right now, take a look around your mind, and write down all the things you would want if you could wave a magic wand and have them instantly:

1. _____

2. _____

3. _____

4. _____

5. _____

6. _____

Remember this: By letting go of wanting, we allow ourselves to have.

So, we've talked about the theory. Now what other technique can we use to get rid of the baggage, so we can have whatever we choose? We'll start by filling out the table below.

From the list of things you wrote above, pick one thing, and put it at the top of the table on page 67. Notice how instead of saying 'I want...' we phrase this as 'I allow myself to have...' This puts it into the affirmative, and means we are not reinforcing the lack every time we work on this statement. Saying 'I allow' is also very passive. It assumes that when you stop putting energy into resisting it, or wanting it, the natural state is for you to have it.

Once you've decided what it is you're going to work on letting go of, fill out a reason why you want it. Can you see this as either wanting love, wanting to control or change something, or wanting security? Just make a note of that in the second column. Then move to the third column and ask yourself the following three questions:

1. Could you let it go?

2. If you could, would you?

3. When would be a good time?

When you've let it go, tick the column next to it and then ask yourself another reason why you want it, and repeat the process. Keep going until nothing else comes to mind.

I allow myself to have:_____
(Fill out the 'want' here, e.g., a new Lamborghini.)

Reasons I want it	Wanting love, wanting control, wanting security?	Let it go?
Nice to drive		
Friends will think I'm cool		
Strangers will think I'm cool		
Can impress clients		
Reasons I resist having it	Wanting love, wanting control, wanting security?	Let it go?
Not very economical		
Fuel is expensive		
Massive insurance premium		
Bad for environment		
Expensive if I crash it		
Will probably crash it because I'm precious about it		
Tricky to park		

Now, in the first column of the lower part of the table, write down a reason why you think you are resisting having it. For example, you may not think you are worthy of having it; you may not truly want it; you may think you are silly for wanting it in the first place. Whatever reason first comes to mind, jot it down and then let it go in the same way as you did with the first three columns.

When you've done that, go to the next row down and start filling out your next reason for wanting it. Keep filling in the rows on your grid until you have no feelings about this item one way or the other. At this point you can just allow yourself to have it. Then move on to the next thing on your list.

What you will find is that over the next few weeks you will start to recognize that you are either better off not having something, or it will just magically show up in your world, effortlessly, without you needing to give it any more thought.

You can download a free supplementary audio recording of this process in a guided meditation, specifically for attracting more money, at www.wireyourselfforwealth.com

Let's now look at some frequently asked questions and answers about the releasing process.

How many 'wants' are associated with each thing I write down?

It may be one, a combination of a couple of them, or all three. The thing to do is write down which it is, then work through the releasing questions in sequence for each individual want, giving yourself the opportunity to let go of each one separately.

What exactly is 'wanting love'?

This is a feeling associated with not feeling good enough – or feeling inferior to how you should be or how everyone else around you is. Because this is something that we don't necessarily think about or talk about in everyday conversations, it may not be immediately apparent to us.

It is also the category of want associated with feelings of disapproval – either with ourselves, or with someone else. If you notice you are disapproving of someone or something, let go of the feeling of disapproval, and then send them/it some love. This releases the 'lack-of-love' feeling from your system. If you find yourself disapproving of yourself, remember it is also an illusion that you lack love for yourself. Once you can allow your feelings of disapproval to leave, you will realize more and more that love is all there is. Nothing you do will ever result in you not *having* love. You *are* love. And there is *nothing but* love. The idea that there is ever an absence of love is just an illusion created by the ego to keep us locked in limitation. It's not real. Or true. So we can just let it go.

What if I don't want to let it go?

Normally this will show up on the second question: 'If you could let it go, would you?' If this comes up for you, it's smart to recognize that whatever it is you're holding on to is causing your 'stuckness.' This is the time to be your own coach and say: 'Okay, maybe my ego is taking me for a ride because I want to be right, or because I want to maintain control, or because I don't want to feel uncomfortable.' Then you need to explain to yourself that if you don't allow yourself to feel uncomfortable briefly, you will never be able to progress and move on. So, then it comes to decision time – do you want to remain exactly as you are and hang on to all the stuff that's holding you back and making you tired and less effective, or would you like to let it go and move on?

You may say that you don't want to let it go because another person hurt you and you don't want to let them off the hook. This is quite natural as a first reaction. However, because you're smart and committed to yourself and the evolution of your consciousness, you will probably realize quite quickly that there is no way at all that hanging on to an emotion is going to punish someone else. Staying mad, hurt, or judgmental only ever damages *you* – and affects your energetic bodies and eventually your physical tissue, too.

What about feeling good? Surely you're not telling me to let go of that?

The choice is always yours, but it's worth considering that underneath the good feelings there are often more uncomfortable ones that we hold on to. When we hold on, we're suppressing, and if we're suppressing we are wasting massive amounts of effort and energy. If you stop releasing emotions and thoughts when you feel good, you'll only ever scrape the surface.

The other thing is that feeling good is often a distraction the ego uses in order to maintain control and distract you from doing the releasing work. It will tell you 'Oh, I feel okay now. I'm not really bothered about such and such anymore, so I can stop doing this work.' That way your ego gets to hang on to all the other baggage around it without really letting go of the whole issue. It won't be long before this resonance pattern manifests in the physical world and gives you another situation to deal with that will make you feel exactly the same way as you did before. So it's better to take it all out – both good and bad.

Does this mean that ultimately I'll never be able to feel good?

No – not at all! The very reason you're doing this releasing process is so that you can feel joyous and peaceful all the time. You get to a point where you're never holding on to anything anymore, so you're constantly in release. Letting go always feels blissful. Just remember, the more stuff you let go of, the freer and happier you are within your soul.

It's always your choice as to whether you let go or not. You can't do it without making the decision to let go, but why would you hold onto a thought or a feeling that makes you miserable? Or one that stands in the way of you having everything as you would love it to be, as easily as clicking your fingers?

Now that you have tackled all the things that have been holding you back, in the next chapter you will start learning the positive steps you need to take to wire yourself for wealth.

Points to Remember

- Emotional baggage and the limiting decisions we make are our only obstacles

- Without the baggage we can have whatever we choose

- Emotions should be felt and released, not numbed

- Your intention creates your world

Let's now move on to the third key – discovering your Money Genius type.

Chapter 4
Key 3: Find Your Money Genius Type

So far we've been covering the foundations – those things you need to have in place to be in a position to cultivate your wealth garden. Now it's time to start landscaping. That's right – we're talking about mapping what you want your landscape to look like: it's strategy time. This is where we focus on the things you need to take action on to wire yourself for wealth.

The first of these is that you need to find out where your Money Genius lies because, as I mentioned briefly in Chapter 1, each of us has a little Money Genius sitting in the corner of our minds. And each Genius type (also known as your Wealth Profile) has a different strategy it excels at to generate cash.

There are eight Money Genius types, offering eight different ways to effortless fun and inspired wealth. Yes, only eight! Anything you can think of is just a variation on one of these eight. This is good news, because it means that if you know your Money Genius type, you automatically know with surgical precision which strategy you should be using in your business and your day-to-day activities to maximize your results. You also know which role models you should be looking to emulate by adopting their strategies and adapting them to your own work.

Knowing where your strengths lie, you can tweak your job role and your career path to maximize your results and your best chance of success. If you're self-employed or you run your own business, this is even more vital in staying ahead of your competition and absolutely loving what you do.

But, unless you know what your profile is, and thus what works for you, the odds are you're going to find making, and keeping, money an uphill struggle. You see, when you're stressed out, or bored, or overwhelmed, the odds are you are playing 'off-profile.' You'll spend everything you make, and whatever you make will be hard work. But when everything is flowing and happening effortlessly, you are playing 'on profile' – that is, you're playing to the strengths of your profile.

The best way to appreciate this is to understand that there are lots of diverse wealth strategies, and they all seemingly pull you in different directions.

Which Path to Wealth?

Imagine landing on the beautiful shores of Opportunity Bay, with numerous routes to paradise at the center of the island called Life. You realize you are truly blessed to have so many possible paths to financial freedom and success. But as you set off along one path, you start to wonder whether another path would be quicker, easier, or sweeter. Your excitement and optimism slowly turn to discontent. To frustrate you further, numerous guides and vendors appear along the way, hassling and cajoling you to take their route over any other.

All routes look idyllic, and all have the potential to get you where you need to go, as each guide can show you postcards from people who have made it to their individual paradise by following the route they propose. The thing is you feel overwhelmed and as if you are being pulled from pillar to post, each step becoming less and less decisive, each moment more doubtful, wondering if you are really doing the right thing. Life was good back on those golden shores of Opportunity Bay. Why couldn't you have just stayed there?

Eventually you find yourself *paralyzed by indecision* and *frustrated by wasted efforts* trying to make progress along your chosen path. You sit down on a nearby rock to contemplate your next move. When you don't know the best path for you, an abundance of possibilities is really a curse.

You know what I'm talking about, right? Even though things may be going well for you at the moment, I'm sure you can identify with this difficulty. This is the situation most of us face when battling to decide how to generate our wealth – whether in property, internet marketing, stock trading, investment, or any other type of opportunity.

Switching from one path to another starts to wear thin, and eventually we wonder if we will ever get to our destination. We try different routes, never knowing which one is truly right for us. When we hit problems we tend to get upset with ourselves, or try again, and slip in and out of our natural Flow on Optimism Rollercoaster.

Having all these different paths is a lot like having many different games to play. You see, you wouldn't get Donald Trump playing the wealth game in the same way as Bill Gates; nor would Oprah Winfrey use the same wealth-generating approach as Warren Buffett or Larry Page. Each has a different strategy, or type of thing they do, to generate wealth in the best way *for them*. The thing is, they know their strengths and stick to them, and so they do the same thing over and over again, each time leveraging more.

What if You Knew Exactly which Game You Needed to Play to Make Money Easily?

If you knew that, you could say a cheery 'No, thank you', to all the other opportunities, and focus on just *learning the rules* and *honing the skills* of that one Game. Then, all of a sudden, overwhelm turns into absolute *clarity* and *focus*.

Wealth Profiling, or more specifically Wealth Dynamics, is a system of profiling entrepreneurs (and aspiring entrepreneurs) developed by social entrepreneur Roger Hamilton. Roger is a co-founder of the XL Group, the first international network dedicated to social entrepreneurship, which brings social entrepreneurs together to share resources, knowledge, and connections.

In studying the specifics of the strategies used by some of the world's most wealthy and successful entrepreneurs, Roger discovered that they could be boiled down to just eight unique, separate strategies.

That's right... *there are just eight basic ways in which to create wealth.*

What's more, he also noticed there was a sequence or a rhythm to these different strategies, which correlated to a pattern in the personality attributes of the wealth creators using the strategies. Laying them out in a sequence, which we will later explore as the Wealth Profile matrix, he noticed there were similarities between the energies of the strategies and people, and the ancient Chinese oracle, the *I Ching*.

The *I Ching* is 5,000 years old and it was used for divination purposes. But it also contains ancient wisdom written down by generations and generations of emperors. Within it are many themes and cycles, which once understood can shed new light and clarity on life's path.

The oracle recognizes there is a natural ebb and flow to everything, from the seasons to the economy, from relationships to our own spiritual journey. Everything goes through cycles. Everything changes constantly. Indeed the *I Ching* is also known as the *Book of Change*. This information is incredibly useful to us as it gives us the power to recognize the seasons of change so that we can adapt to stay in Flow.

Used correctly Wealth Dynamics offers an excellent starting point for developing wealth whilst respecting our spiritual nature – because, as you will discover, the techniques and principles all act to keep us in our natural Flow. And in Flow, we only ever do what comes naturally and effortlessly to us, which helps us get deeper into our personal Money Mojo.

There are eight profiles and each of us has one primary profile. The eight profiles are named as follows: Creator, Star, Supporter, Deal Maker, Trader, Accumulator, Lord, and Mechanic.

We will discuss each one in more detail in Chapter 5, but first I'd like to explain a bit more about Wealth Profiling.

Why Is Wealth Profiling So Useful?

Knowing your Wealth Profile is invaluable because through it you know not only which strategy you need to use to create wealth easily for your personality type, but also which things you *shouldn't* be doing.

For the longest time I wanted to be a Trader. Even though I knew I was a Star profile (which is almost as far away as you can get from a Trader profile), I still wanted to trade the financial markets.

And for a while I did well. I did options trading, Forex trading, as well as position trading on the FTSE, but each time I got into a strategy, I'd get bored. Getting up early in the morning to trade became a drag, a chore. And so, what started as four mornings a week scheduled for trading, became three mornings, then two mornings, until it slipped to once every couple of weeks.

Do you think I wasted a lot of energy thinking I should be trading, but not having the energy to do it? Do you think I beat myself up over having the keys to make money, but not following it through? You bet I did. The point was I wasn't in Flow. I wasn't doing what came naturally to my profile. I was operating off-profile.

Since then I have met several Star profiles who dabbled in trading – some successfully by most people's standards, but all of whom gave up when they realized that there are easier ways to make money... namely, in front of a group of people, creating a brand, and loving every minute of it. So the beauty of knowing your game, and adhering to it, means that you don't end up in a rut doing tasks that you don't enjoy. Instead you're able to focus your efforts working on activities that light you up and fulfill you. You get to be 'in Flow'.

Why Is It So Important to Be Doing What You Love?

Money is money, right? Wrong! When you need money, it is easy to fall in to the belief that you need to do anything to get money and that getting more money will make all the bad stuff go away. This is seldom the case. When you're desperate to get more money, the energy is wrong. You resonate at low-level energy, and attract more of the same low-energy luck and results. You literally create a negative outcome because you are trying so hard.

Often I come across individuals who are desperate to make more money quickly. Sometimes they have their back against the wall with their home about to be repossessed; sometimes they've just lost their job, or are unable to work. In this place they'll invest in all kinds of programs in the hope that this will be their ticket to a more comfortable life. However, they rarely experience the degree of success they dreamed of when they signed on the dotted line simply because they are working against themselves by trying to make *any old thing* work. They end up back where they started, only more in debt and more disillusioned. This is the 'any-port-in-a-storm' strategy – and it doesn't work.

What I often suggest is to stack the odds in your favor. When you know your profile, only take up the opportunities that you have the best chance of sticking with and loving – not because they give you the money you may need or desire, but because you love to do those things anyway.

The other great thing about knowing your profile is that you immediately know which tasks you *shouldn't* be doing and therefore, who else you need around you to be doing them *for* you. Just because *you* might hate paperwork, for instance, doesn't mean that someone else will not absolutely love it. For example, being organized and completing tasks is what comes naturally to Traders and Lords, but Creators really struggle with it. On the other hand, getting started and seeing the bigger picture is something that *is* within the Flow of a Creator profile.

So, knowing all this, what's the sensible thing to do? Change how you operate, of course! For example, if you're a Creator who already has a business, your best game plan is to get someone else to manage the day-to-day running of the business, leaving you free to create and work on the business. I thoroughly recommend having Trader profiles for getting things done. They are so efficient when they get going. Mechanics are also great, because they can be so process-driven that they are outstanding at implementing systems and processes that a business needs to run. They create the 'running order' that everyone else in an enterprise adheres to in order to sell and deliver.

You may not have a team around you yet. You may be reading this thinking that to get a team around you is a big job and more than you are ready for right now. Apart from anything, how on earth are you going to pay for a team? This is something every business has to overcome as it moves from a concept to an entity in its own right, and the way it happens is that someone somewhere along the line gets really passionate about what the service or product can do for people.

This passion is seriously attractive. Correctly directed with clear vision and purpose, this passion will attract the right individuals to you. You won't necessarily have to pay a salary to make this happen. Most projects on a small scale are run by splitting profits when there are some, and done more as a labor of love in the first stage. Don't worry about *how* you're going to attract a team for now. Sit tight and find out about *who* you need and we'll come to the *when*, *where*, and *how* later.

Now that we know how important it is to be in our own Flow, let's talk about what exactly Flow is – and more importantly what it's *not*.

Force versus Flow

I ran a Facebook competition to define 'Flow', and these were just some of the answers submitted:

- *'Experience, Allow and Trust... equals Flow.'*

- *'Flow: That continuous moment when you realize that time has stopped and you are so easily content with your very existence.'*

- *'A natural, easy, nonresistant allowance of motion from one state to the next, to the next, to the next, always moving, never hurried, never slowing – just flowing.'*

- *'Flow is when there is fluency and precision that gives an effortless result.'*

- *'Flow is what happens when human will meets up with Divine will.'*

- *'Flow is defined as a series of perfect moments joined together.'*

These are all fantastic definitions. I like the last one simply because it presupposes that you are living in the moment.

Let's read that again: 'Flow is defined as a series of perfect moments joined together.' You may have heard it said that your power is in the present moment, and later in this book you will discover that when your energy is invested in the past, or the future, you weaken your ability to either operate or manifest in the present.

Healers have to practice remaining present all the time in order to build up huge stores of energy to facilitate healing. Being present in the here and now is also the first essential step to being in Flow. This means we need to drop the worrying and the beating ourselves up about the past. All that counts right now is the present moment!

It is also important that we understand the difference between *force* and *Flow*, as this actually cuts through to the very foundations of implementing our Wealth Profile. When we are *in Flow*, doing what comes easily to us and lights us up, everything is much more enjoyable, easier, requires less effort, and gives us significantly better results. To use a sports analogy, do you think that if Tiger Woods was forcing his game, rather than flowing with the play, he would be nearly as effective? Does he use a lot of power sometimes? Of course he does. But power is different from force. Power is what is needed to break a board with a fist; force tends to result in a broken hand.

This is a distinction that will serve us well when we come up against obstacles. If something is difficult and hard work it probably means that you're using force, not Flow – that is, you are working off-profile, and doing something your inner Money Genius just isn't suited to. When you are stressed out and working hard, you are doing tasks that are off-profile, things that don't come naturally to you. This is the opposite of being in Flow, and doing tasks that are on-profile – things that *do* come naturally to you.

You've probably experienced times when you were making money and having a fantastic time. Even if you were 'working' ridiculously long hours, time seemed to fly and you'd have felt sad to stop. Getting out of bed in the morning was effortless and you walked with a spring in your step. This was the time when you were totally in Flow. This was when your Money Mojo was in full swing.

....

EXERCISE: RECALLING FLOW

Take a moment now and recall a time when you were in Flow. Note down the tasks you were doing; the interactions you had with people; how you felt; whether you were in a team or working alone; if you were making the decisions or leaving that to someone else. Also write down what you notice you were *not* doing and see if there is a pattern there, too.

All these things give you clues and help you work out what types of tasks bring you into a state of Flow. Once you have an idea of this, it's simple to spend more time doing the things that you do when you are in Flow, and delegate or outsource the rest.

....

The Wealth–Profile Matrix

In the following section we are going to look at the Wealth-Profile matrix as a whole, before breaking it down and exploring each of the eight individual profiles in Chapter 5.

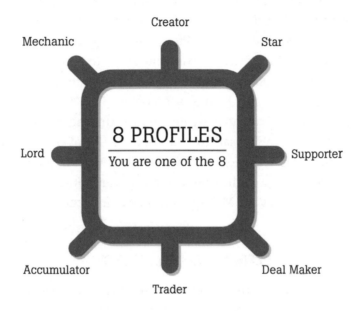

Figure 4.1: Matrix showing the 8 Wealth Profiles

As you read through this section think about which traits and characteristics apply to you – this will help you to identify your own profile.

The first distinction to make is that, in very broad terms, on the right-hand side of the diagram we have the extroverts and on the left-hand side, the introverts.

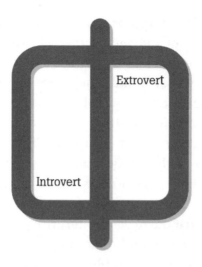

Figure 4.2: The profile matrix: introverts vs. extroverts

More than this though, those who fall into the categories on the right-hand side tend to be people-orientated, while those on the left-hand side are better focusing on systems.

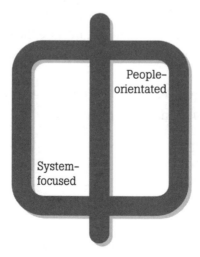

Figure 4.3: The profile matrix: people-orientated vs. system-focused

If we take the **Supporter** profile in the center of the right-hand side of the square (see Figure 4.1 above) as an example, we find that these guys are the most people-focused folks you will find. They have huge networks of friends, acquaintances, and colleagues. Directly opposite on the left-hand side we have the **Lord** profile. To these individuals people aren't a priority. They would much rather sit and analyse a system, a process, or data, with a view to making logical decisions to improve it. These attributes are key to the way in which Supporters and Lords will contribute to your enterprise or team.

Additionally we find that on the right-hand side, the people-orientated profiles tend toward leveraging through magnifying the message, the product, or the service. They take the initial concept, develop it, and make it bigger. By contrast, on the left-hand side of the matrix everything is reduced to its simplest possible form and leverages out by multiplying it lots of times. This is the difference between commanding a big fee for something that is a valuable brand, and making something easily replicable so that it can be easily distributed in the marketplace.

Next, we will examine two other extremes: Intuitive thinking versus sensory knowledge.

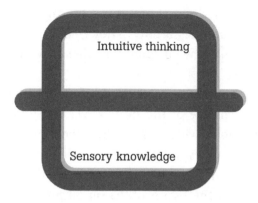

Figure 4.4: The division between intuitive thinking and sensory knowledge

At the top of the matrix in Figure 4.1, you have the profiles of people who have high-frequency energies and are 'blue-sky', creative thinkers. They are plugged in from above and are constantly pulling down ideas from goodness knows where! These guys find implementation tricky, mostly because as soon as they start something, they tend to have another deluge of ideas they also want to develop.

Creators are the embodiment of this energy: they have too many ideas too quickly, and struggle ever to get any of them implemented. They have a constant stream of ideas and insights and get frustrated because the people around them struggle to keep up with them. Gaining clarity and traction in a niche is essential for Creators.

Traders, on the other hand, who are found at the bottom of the diagram (Figure 4.1) directly opposite Creators, are very grounded and have an incredible sense of timing. They know what is going on at any time and live in the moment. They are concerned with getting lots of things done, one after the other. Having their 'finger on the pulse' is one of their key phrases.

The profiles situated along the bottom of the matrix represent 'what is, right now'. They're not concerned with 'what has been' or 'what could be'– these are questions for other profiles.

Now that we have covered the four profiles that are placed at each side of the matrix, we can go on to look at the other four, which sit on the corners of the square. There is a certain evolution to this Money Genius profiling matrix. Those on the corners almost embody a mixture of the energies of the two profiles on either side. However, unlike a physical reaction when you mix salt and water together to get a saline solution (which can be separated out again), the profile energies chemically combine to make new profiles. These new profiles have distinct characteristics and associated strategies, far different from the component energies making them up. We will explore these and all the individual profiles in more detail in the next chapter.

Crime-Scene Investigation

So how exactly does profiling work? Let's start with a bit of background. To do this, I like to compare it to criminal profiling. We've all seen this kind of thing on TV. The advent of the *CSI* series, *NCIS*, *Criminal Minds*, the *X-Files*, as well as any number of movies on our screens, has demonstrated the process that profilers go through in order to catch serial killers and criminals.

Generally the case starts at the Scene of Crime. This is where the investigators gather clues about what happened and who was involved. They also profile the victim, as they are generally a known quantity. Taking this information the investigators then use their vast knowledge and insights into criminal behavior in order to build a profile of the kind of person that could have committed the act.

The key lies in piecing together the collection of information gathered to get a personality profile. The way this is determined is by analysing huge amounts of data from previous criminals who have committed similar acts. You see, prior to this event happening, investigators have spent huge amounts of time interviewing criminals, and correlating crime scenes with the victims so that they can predict with varying degrees of certainty what type of killer commits what type of crime. When they have the crime scene and victim information to go on, it becomes relatively easy to work backward and produce a highly accurate profile of the personality of the perpetrator.

The same principles were applied to produce the eight Wealth Profiles – except in this case, we're profiling you for your best and most effective path to accumulate wealth. Using the same methods as those used to analyse serial killers and their crime scenes, Roger Hamilton, who created Wealth Dynamics, studied a number of incredibly successful people, and their 'crime scenes' – their empires or their business enterprises. Mapping the correlation between the role they played in their own success, their personality type, and their *modus operandi* (in this case, the wealth strategy they used), he discovered a number of patterns.

These are the correlations that are mapped when you take the profile test. We look at your crime scene (your past and present money successes and failures), and your personality and from these deduce what your most effective and successful path to money will be.

A really good place to start is to consider any projects you've 'failed' at. You've probably heard 'there's no such thing as failure,' only feedback. So looking at the tasks and projects you've undertaken that fall into this category of feedback is immensely useful in discovering your innate value. Why? Because it is such fertile territory, rich in information about which profile strategies will *not* work for you. The more you can understand where your Flow *isn't*, the more you will be able to monitor what you do, so that you focus on the things you excel at.

With this in mind, spend some time and write down all the times you've been involved in a project that didn't make you any money. Examine the strategies you used and be honest with yourself as to whether you felt it was fun or just plain hard work. We will come back to this list when we go through the individual profiles, and you start to flesh out your understanding of where your Money Genius really lies.

Now read the primary characteristics and skills of the profiles below and keep in mind the tasks you were doing when you were succeeding at making money. This is a very good guide to understanding what your primary profile may be, and therefore which strategy you should employ in future ventures.

Creator

- Head in the clouds

- Distracted by a constant stream of ideas

- Too many ideas to implement

- Difficulties in actually bringing ideas to fruition

Strategies that have probably worked for you in terms of making money:

- Creating products or content

- Inventing things

- Writing stories; courses

- Making films; all forms of design

- Coaching and consulting

Star

- Loves exciting, new, shiny things

- Likes to have an audience

- Appearance and image very important

- Outgoing and confident in front of groups of people

Strategies that have probably worked for you include:

- Sales jobs, promoting products and services

- Anything that requires building attention in a market-place/with an audience

- Anything in front of a camera

- Building something that depends heavily on brand

Supporter

- Great at communicating with people

- A 'people collector'

- Genuine interest and love of people

- Great at building a team in which everyone is happy and productive

Strategies that have probably worked for you in terms of making money include:

- Anything in which you've had to manage a team and get the best out of people

- Taking tasks away from the wealth creator to free up their flow

- Networking to find clients and valuable business contacts

Deal Maker

- Always takes calls, very accessible, afraid to miss an opportunity

- Generally feels guilty about spending time with people doing deals because they find it so easy

- Great in front of customers, and pulling necessary people into a business/deal

Strategies which have probably worked for you in terms of making money include:

- Being able to bring the right people and resources together

- Making money in individual deals and transactions, e.g. sale of a property

- Anything that involves a negotiation

- Connecting an individual up to a market/audience/ organization

- Being a conduit

Trader

- Has ear to the ground

- Concerned only with what is current; very grounded and present

- More stressed when nothing to do

- Great at implementing things and 'getting stuff done'

- Likes to follow a system set up by someone else

Strategies that have probably worked for you in terms of making money include:

- Making money out of margins, trading

- Getting lots of things done for someone else

- Handling lots of transactions at one time

- Transactional sales

- Caring, nursing, nurturing

Accumulator

- Likes to accumulate objects, ideas, information, knowledge

- Collectors

- Good at building asset portfolio: property, databases, Twitter contacts – anything that could be useful, and sometimes things that never will be

- Good at accumulating cash

- Great at analysing data

Strategies that have probably worked for you in terms of making money include:

- Selling assets that you have been collecting

- Generating cash out of assets you own (e.g. rental properties, holiday homes etc)

- Research, and analysing information

Lord

- Good at controlling assets which bring cash

- Great with research and fine detail

- Great at squeezing margins out of existing businesses and/or systems

- Cautious, measured approach

Strategies that have probably worked for you in terms of making money include:

- Analysing and managing information

- Making tweaks to systems to make them more profitable

- Managing cash; keeping a rein on expenses and outgoings

- Controlling/owning cash-producing assets

Mechanic

- Great at tinkering with and improving systems

- Loves processes, systems

- Understands easily how things work

Strategies that have probably worked for you in terms of making money include:

- Tweaking other people's systems, businesses

- Making things work

- Being able to work through spreadsheets of data and make refinements

- Creating systems and then franchising them

If you'd like to find out about your profile in more depth, head on over to my website where you'll be walked through an exercise and can download a worksheet that will help you analyse your own personal crime scene. Just pop over to www.wireyourselfforwealth.com now.

Niche and Network

Once you know your best path to wealth, is this enough? No – this is why we have seven keys to the process. But part of this third key is really accepting your profile and making the necessary changes.

This means a few things. The first is that you act on your profile. You let go of doing the things that don't fit with your strategy to wealth – the things your Money Genius doesn't do well. You delegate them, reassign them, get resourceful – anything to get them off your plate so you can focus on what you excel at.

The second is that you find your niche. Even when you know what kinds of things you should be doing, you need to pick an area or an industry you want to operate in. You can't just jump from one industry to another, or any value in the network you accumulate will be lost with all the chopping and changing. You need to become known in *one* industry for *one* thing, and to become the person folks go to for that particular thing.

The third thing is partly related to your niche, but has more to do with the relationships you have with people in your niche. This is your network. You need to cultivate a network of people you can call upon to connect you to the resources you need in your transmutation of stuff into wealth. It doesn't matter which profile you are, no one can work in isolation. Every profile needs other profiles around them, and other people and resources in order to convert their intrinsic value into cash. Remember the discussion about having a Vehicle of Value Conversion (see page 6)? This is the same principle. Your network needs to be there to help you manifest something out of it that will eventually translate into cash.

Confused? Disappointed? Excited? Scared?

By now you have probably been over to www.wireyourselfforwealth.com to discover what your profile is.

I remember one guy who took his profile and came out as a Mechanic. When he understood the powerful traits of a Mechanic profile he felt a huge burden had been lifted from him. All his life he had found that he was naturally able to improve things, from his friend's drawings at kindergarten to other people's computer systems, to the barbecuing process at parties, but he just became stuck whenever he tried to create something of his own from scratch.

When he realized that his Flow and value were not in creating something from the beginning, but in his ability to improve things that were already there, he excelled, moving from various freelancing jobs, to a directorship in a well-known computer software company. He started thriving.

How did *you* feel when you discovered your profile? If you felt a mixture of emotions when you found out which type you are, you are not alone. Some people feel it is an anticlimax; some feel that it's not who they are. Some have an immediate recognition and an 'a-ha' moment, whilst others wonder immediately how their profile affects what they are doing in their business. Some people feel a huge release. Whatever you feel – it's okay.

Points to Remember

- There are eight Money Genius types or Wealth Profiles, each of which has its own best strategy for creating wealth

- Knowing your profile allows you to say no to the things that aren't in your Flow

- Defining your niche is vital to creating your wealth

- Attract a network of people in your niche to help you

In the next chapter we will explore each profile individually and examine the strategies each excels at so that you can ignite your Money Genius and crank your Money Mojo up a gear!

Chapter 5
The Eight Money Genius Profiles

As we've already seen in Chapter 4, there are eight Money Genius types or Wealth Profiles. Everyone is primarily one profile. A person's profile doesn't *fundamentally* change over time, though the outcome of the profile test may shift slightly depending on the answers you give, which might vary due to the tasks that you are undertaking at the time of the test. For example, if you're spending more time going out selling your services, and less time creating products, you may answer more as a Star than a Creator profile. But the more you're working to your natural strengths, the lower the probability of this distortion occurring.

The great thing is once you know your profile, you know which money game you should always play – no matter what. Though you may get distracted and bend and flex in response to demands made upon you, if you wish to remain successful you will keep coming back to the strategy of your true Money Genius.

When Warren Buffett took a public speaking course he said it was not to prevent his knees from knocking when speaking publicly, but to undertake public speaking whilst his knees *were* knocking. Buffett is a Lord profile. He will always be a Lord profile. This is where his genius lies. He may be called upon to assume the Star role and speak to shareholders from time to time, but his Flow is in the detail of companies. And this is what he generally sticks to.

So let's now turn our attention to discover more about the characteristics of each profile, and the strategies each should employ in order to get into their Flow.

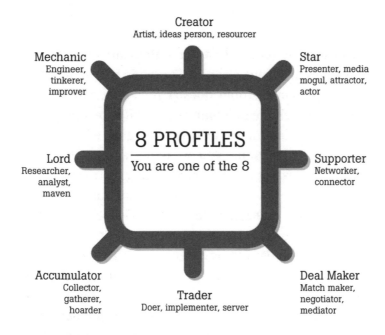

Figure 5.1: Matrix showing the 8 Money Genius profiles

Creator (artist, ideas person, resourcer)

'Creating a better product'

Creators are renowned for having their head in the clouds. Characteristically they have too many ideas at once. This is why we could also label the profile as the 'Artist' or 'Ideas Person.' At lower energies (or early phases of development) procrastination often creeps in because they can't get going on one idea as they are constantly interrupted by other brainwaves. Choosing which enterprise to be in or which course of action to take can be their biggest obstacle.

Even at higher energies, Creators are easily distracted and need to adopt strategies for deciding where their focus should go at any one time.

Creators, whilst often geniuses, are terrible at completing and following their projects through. They need a team to implement their ideas. Thus the Creators who really have mastered living in their profile realize that they shouldn't be involved in the mundane running of the business. As quickly as possible they need to extract themselves from the day-to-day, process-driven detail and work on the bigger picture.

Simultaneously, they need to maintain a structure and form a team around themselves to carry out the tasks that are not their strong points. Even with this in place the Creator's biggest challenge and frustration occurs when their team can't keep up with them. As such, the Creator needs to filter what they communicate to other profiles, who are often overwhelmed by their speed of thought and the fear of having to implement everything they speak about.

Some comfort will be offered to the other profiles in understanding that when a Creator speaks, it is often just a way of running their ideas past their own internal scanner. The person listening may be their Operations Manager or PA but really, until the idea has taken root, decisive action has been taken, and some work has been done on it, the listener is just acting as a sounding board. Most entrepreneurs I come across operate from this profile (either in a primary or secondary capacity).

Trying to get a Creator profile to hone down on minute detail is like trying to drag an elephant out of quicksand. It's a far more effective use of time and energy to allow the Creator profile to do what they do best and pull together the right people and resources constructively. They can then let someone whose passion is dealing with detail attend to it. This is *not* the same as washing your hands of the detail, though.

A downfall of the Creator who hasn't yet learnt to harness their profile is that they get really good at saying the detail isn't their concern, and thus never progress beyond the blue-sky thinking. One of the greatest challenges entrepreneurs face, after focus, is being able to go into enough detail to be able to brief another person sufficiently to enable them to go away and sort out a problem.

For example, I could say to my copywriter that I need a piece that's going to advertise one of my courses online, and expect her to come up with the detail. But, as good as she is, that's just not enough information for a brief. It won't yield results. I have to take responsibility for telling her exactly what the benefits of the course are, what my perfect client looks like, what stage of personal development they are at, and why they need the course. Then she has the detail with which to go away and write something meaningful. Continuing this as the example, does this mean I then micromanage everything she writes and correct her grammar? No, *that* detail is her responsibility and, left to it, she takes pride in her work. She won't ever submit anything that is third rate, as she knows that everything she produces is a reflection of her talent and not the 'job function' she performs. So you see, being a Creator still holds some responsibility for detail – but the right kind of detail.

This is a fine example of the power of wealth profiling because it demonstrates the importance of according the correct responsibilities to individuals to give them free rein to be as enterprising as they can be.

One famous, successful Creator was Steve Jobs. He was a Creator in essence, but he also used the Star and Mechanic profiles as and when he needed to. He certainly played the Star when he stood on stage in front of press and employees and announced his next vision for Apple. He also showed his Mechanic profile when he made the decision that Apple needed to develop a mechanism to control an MP3 player with only the thumb, thus giving birth to the innovative control on the iPod. Note that Steve Jobs, like many Creators, operated midway between people and systems, bridging the gap between the two. The presence of a Creator profile also ensures the enterprise is able to develop and reinvent itself as required.

The key task for a Creator is to find a market niche that they can dominate and then pull together the resources to get the product or service to the market quickly. In some ways it is appropriate to also call this profile a Resourcer, as their job is to bring the resources together in a creative way.

Finding the right niche is key here. Virgin boss Richard Branson attempted to enter the cola market with Virgin Cola, but his competitor was just so huge that the company could easily afford to pay their sales force to follow his people from one store to another and push them out of the market. This wasn't a niche he could dominate and so he was eventually forced to withdraw.

Which niche could you dominate? To raise your effectiveness as a Creator profile the first things you need to do are:

1. Decide what you really want out of an enterprise. What do you want it to give you? How many hours do you wish to work? What kind of lifestyle would you like?

2. Find and define a market niche you can dominate.

3. Get your stream of ideas down onto paper.

4. Assess each idea based on your desired outcomes (as in point 1), how easy it is to achieve those, how big the likely obstacles are, and so on. Essentially you want to perform a cost/benefit/achievability analysis on each idea in turn, ranking them in order of likeliness. You want to be able to identify quickly which are likely to be the easiest to implement.

5. Pick one idea to focus on for the next 90 days.

6. Make a list of all possible resources available to you.

7. Talk to people in your chosen field.

8. Find a Supporter profile in your niche to hook you up with the expertise and resources you need to implement your chosen idea.

9. Keep going back and assessing which ideas are worth pursuing and which you need to let go of to allow yourself time, energy, and head space to pursue the ones that matter right now.

Star (presenter, media mogul, attractor, actor)

'Creating a unique brand'

Star profiles take the shoots of the Creator's ideas from where they have grown, and turn them into a tree. Stars are great at sales as they are good at making the same presentation again and again, no matter how repetitive. Those who succeed are the ones who constantly strive to improve their delivery and closure rate. In this way they can also be seen as presenters and excellent salespeople.

Stars are often more comfortable on a platform than in a one-to-one interaction. The energy and attention of the crowd makes them witty, creative, and entertaining. They thrive on attention. Other words embodying the Star profile include 'attractor' and even 'actor' as they have a magnetism that people love to watch. Think of any TV or movie star and the quality they display on camera and you'll immediately see the essence of the Star profile's power.

People with star profiles also have the ability to improvise: on the one hand they can think on their feet, on the other hand they have a tendency to try and speak or perform without preparing, with varying results. However, professional Stars relish the preparation. They will prepare their presentation, research their audience or prospect, and will keep good records. This is one aspect that separates successful sales professionals from hustlers (who always get found out and are therefore constantly trying to find new people to hustle).

The Star's strength lies in shining a light and attracting people to that beacon. This light is a way of magnifying, rather than multiplying, whatever they promote. By contrast an example of multiplying would be to launch a product through a huge distribution channel such as Amazon, rather than the Star doing a TV interview about it. The TV interview is another example of magnification in the marketplace.

People whose primary profile is the Star are well suited to brand and marketing strategies that involve the media. If this is your profile you have an excellent opportunity to use the power of TV, YouTube, and radio to promote your message. These are what I call the Media-Mogul attraction strategies.

At low energy Stars are ego-driven with a 'look-at-me' mentality. The ego is always the downfall of the Star profile. Their energy tends to be scattered, flitting from one thing to another as they still retain some of the Creator energy, being tapped into a constant flow of intuitive thinking.

Just like the Creator they need to have a team around to focus them down one course of action and to pick up the detail and running of a business. It is worth mentioning at this point that someone's profile as a Star is not an excuse for them to be a 'prima donna' and avoid doing the hard work. The best Stars go on stage well-informed, well-rehearsed, and well-balanced whether they are comedians, sales professionals, talk-show hosts, presenters, or actors.

To raise their internal frequency from scattered egocentric to superstar with something of value to offer humankind, the Star's first task is to find their voice, and then refine it. Stars need to stand for something. As such, Stars must define their niche. They need to become the authority in an area or consistently promote the same type of products or they will lose credibility. Everyone knows what Oprah stands for – encouraging people to take responsibility for their own lives and creating TV that matters.

Here's my interpretation of what some famous people with Star profiles stand for. Can you think of any others?

- Tony Robbins – empowering individuals to live their best life

- Lady Gaga – giving yourself permission to be who you are, as you are

- Angelina Jolie, one of my all-time heroes – increasing humanitarian aid to the people who need it around the world. The films she makes (beyond the pop-glamor films), the appearances she makes, and humanitarian causes she supports highlight this fact very clearly. She uses her stardom to generate attention for incredible causes such as Peace One Day and UNHCR.

And this is characteristic of a Star in Flow. The Star profile excels at generating the attention, not for themselves but to shine onto a cause or an enterprise. This is where their power lies – in promoting products or services (that they haven't necessarily created), and in getting people to buy in to their personal brand.

A cornerstone of this is that they must foster trust in their brand, but there are many examples of Stars going wrong, and underpinning them is a loss of public trust. As a Star profile, your reputation is your brand, and your brand is your value as a business and as an individual. Protect it.

Stars are great at making lots of money quickly, but are even better at spending it. Consequently they need to team up with someone to hold the purse strings. The other harsh truth that they need to face is that they are not very good negotiators. This is why they must team up with Deal Makers to find the deals and let these experts do the negotiating on their behalf. Moreover, they need to extract themselves as quickly as possible from handling the finances and fees of their enterprise, as this lessens their perceived value very quickly.

To raise your effectiveness as a Star, the first things you need to do are:

1. Define what you stand for – your voice. (Deliberately and consciously refine this as you mature and develop as a Star in business – you want your audience to

see you and your communication evolve between presentations).

2. Always develop your game up to your own high standards – hold yourself accountable for your presentation.

3. Define what you *will* promote, and what you *won't* – that way when your Deal Maker brings you an opportunity, you'll know in advance what will and will not enhance your brand.

4. Gather a team around you so you don't end up negotiating your own fees or getting caught up in your prospects' stories about money and affordability.

5. Make yourself less accessible to maintain your market value. For instance, when booking appointments and meetings, have someone else do it for you. Again, it's not about being a prima donna – if you are operating from this type of energy, people will pick up on it, and you will lose all credibility.

Supporter (networker, connector)

'Leading the team'

The Supporter takes the tree that the Star has grown from the Creator's shoots and creates a red-hot blaze by burning the wood and taking it out into the marketplace through networks.

Supporters have huge networks of people they know. They are purely people-orientated and have little interest in systems – in direct contrast to the Lord profiles on the opposite side of the matrix. What's more they are the glue that holds communities together and connects seemingly separate communities to each other. In this way the Supporter profile could also be called a Connector. They know far more people than the other profiles and are genuinely interested in the people they meet. Now, they may not necessarily become close friends with everyone, but even having met someone just once, they have a connection with that person and are likely to remember them from then on. The Supporters in your team know the names of the kids of your clients, and which school they go to, and who in the client base knows everyone else. They are walking databases of this kind of information and are great at nurturing relationships with people who are valuable to their network.

Their asset is their network, and their value is in the trust that flows through their network. It is the relationships that allow them to make things happen, and ultimately to make money out of their asset. They are great at pulling people together for mutual benefit.

Successful Supporters make great managers, treating each person both as a team member and as an individual. They empower team members and are outstanding at being able to put to best use the skills within their team.

Take Meg Whitman for example (and I thoroughly recommend reading her autobiography if you're a Supporter profile). Whitman is a former CEO of eBay. Her method of leadership embodies the successful

Supporter profile's mentality. Under her leadership, users were empowered to support other users through the message boards. They wrote software and suggested improvements in the way eBay operated. The users of eBay, in the early years especially, were every bit a part of the company's growth as the full-time employees. And this was encouraged. The users also developed a huge loyalty to the company, because when they spoke eBay listened. They were part of the eBay community. They contributed, and they mattered. Whitman also advocated that each employee was unique and had their own talents, and she cultivated a culture where this was recognized by all. Is it any wonder she went on to write a book by the title *The Power of Many?*

By contrast, when they have low energies Supporters are in danger of being social butterflies, knowing people just for the sake of it. They try and put people in touch with each other without gauging what each party needs and don't nurture their network effectively, getting caught up in schemes and groups who aren't working in the same direction. They hope that one day they might be useful and so use a lot of energy trying to maintain extraneous links and connections. In essence, they lack focus. They can also be lacking in integrity and rather than nurturing relationships for everyone's benefit, they see people's worth as only what they can get out of them.

In the same way in which a Star needs to find his voice and refine it, a Supporter needs to define his outcome and develop the network around it. Again, niche is key. This is especially so for Supporters and Deal Makers who, without a niche, find themselves bombarded by people who are irrelevant to the outcome they are trying to achieve, distracting them from cultivating their value. For instance, it would be pointless for a Supporter working in women's clothing retail to try to network with property investors. There would be little mutual benefit.

Successful Supporters leverage their network not by calling through their phone book trying to sell to everyone, but by acting in the best interests of the people they are in contact with. They are selective and protect their network.

Supporters in a team have lots of blazing warm energy and enthusiasm for talking with people. If you have a Supporter on your team you should give them the freedom to build these relationships. However, well-defined criteria and focus are essential or you will have a forest fire on your hands. The Supporters with little direction often end up scattering their focus everywhere and burning out.

To raise your effectiveness as a Supporter profile the first things you need to do are:

1. Define your niche and where you can offer the most value.

2. Spend time with people in that niche and focus primarily on them, even though you may be tempted to go off in other directions on other projects.

3. Find a wealth creator you can support and add value to, in exchange for a share of the profits. Here's the golden nugget: work with someone who is already playing at the level you want to play at.

4. Get out and connect with people in your chosen niche. Mix with them and make yourself useful to people in your network.

5. Take the networking and/or people-management tasks away from the wealth creator to leave them to focus on the core thing that creates the money for the enterprise. Make sure you have agreements in place that ensure you get paid for your contribution and the uplift in profit.

Deal Maker (match maker, negotiator, mediator)

'Bringing people together'

Deal Makers create value through timing not innovation. Their power is in the present and in connecting the right people with the right deals. They are often seen with two or three phones to their ears at any one time. Whilst Stars and Creators maintain their value from limiting access to themselves, the Deal Makers' value comes from making themselves as accessible as possible.

Again, Deal Makers need to define their niche, and stick to it in order to use the powerful connections they can make within their network and attract the deals. They need to become the 'go-to' guy for that niche or more specifically, that type of deal. When they achieve this, the opportunities just pour in.

Let me tell you about Nate, a sales representative at a company that produced interior wall finishes. He was clearly wasted there as he'd previously run a couple of his own companies, and was far more business savvy than the individuals he reported to. Not only that, but he had many contacts in the industry and had a flair for being able to set up partnerships and distribution agreements. This naturally meant he could potentially achieve much more than he could in a normal sales role, simply because his efforts were multiplied through other companies. His counterparts, by contrast, just 'did their job' as prescribed by the company, calling on the company's prospects and customers, often seeing people one at a time.

Can you see the difference in this picture? Nate was skilled at putting together agreements that would ensure that he sold products leveraged off other peoples' efforts as well as his own. He smashed his targets hardly breaking a sweat. However, the commission structure set by the company didn't reward him adequately for the value he could bring in. As his confidence grew, he started attracting better and better opportunities. Eventually he came across the perfect opportunity that would give him the freedom to use his talent more fully. Very soon he found himself looking after the international sales of similar manufacturers, putting together distributor agreements and recruiting his own sales team. His reward was that he got to do something that came more naturally to him and which he could excel at. The financial rewards weren't bad either – he nearly tripled his income overnight! In playing to our strengths and the strategy that best suits our make-up, we are also able to deliver much more value. In doing so, we are in turn rewarded.

Donald Trump is another great example of a Deal Maker. He made his money by being the go-to guy for New York Real Estate. As soon as he started to branch out, no one knew what he stood for and he lost his attraction and even his market share of the New York business being written. He also tried to adopt a Star strategy, running promotions, but this was out of his Flow. When he returned to just doing the deals, as his profile requires, his income recovered.

Deal Makers, like all sensory thinkers, work on what they can observe. As we've already mentioned, their power is in the present and knowing what is happening at that specific time. Staying with the example of New York Real Estate, this applies whether it is knowing who is applying for what planning permission or what the going rate is for a development plot in a particular district; whether it's finding out how many portfolios of properties you can get access to, or how the person on the other side of the negotiation table is responding to your proposal. This information is all current information. Past data and further extrapolation are meaningless to the Money Genius of the Deal Maker profile. Deal Makers need to focus on working with 'what is.'

There is a certain structure to things, as seen by Deal Makers generally. I've heard Deal Makers themselves describe it in workshops as being as if they have two clouds in their head. In these clouds are the things they match up in order to make a deal happen. For example, take David. He matches up commercial properties valued below £1m ($1.6m) with investors who are transitioning from residential to commercial investment. The properties are in one cloud, and the investors are in the other.

To raise your effectiveness as a Deal Maker profile the first things you need to do are:

1. Get very clear on your niche.

2. Define clearly what you do: Whom do you help? Whom do you match up with what? What are in your two clouds? Become the go-to guy for that niche by becoming outstanding. You need to be known for what you do – and known for doing it well.

3. Attract deals – don't chase them.

4. Control the contract and get paid on exchange.

Controlling the contract is important. This is where the value lies for the Deal Maker. One challenge Deal Makers have when they are starting out is insisting on payment on the signing of a contract. As entrepreneurs there is often an understanding that funding is not immediately forthcoming and that taking shares in a business is one way for people to start building a business together. Deal Makers should steer clear of this strategy, as this is not in their Flow. They need to be paid on exchange of contracts in order to extract the value that they bring in making that contract come together. That is what Deal Makers do, and that is what they need to be paid for.

Beyond this, the biggest mindset struggle Deal Makers have is that wining and dining clients and negotiating deals is just so much fun they don't believe that it can count as work. Often I find that they try to work harder by getting bogged down in running the business, which is really something they need to let go and leave to someone else. The Deal Maker's place is out and about attracting and negotiating the deals – networking, building relationships, and bringing home those contracts.

Trader (doer, implementer, server)

'Buy low, sell high'

Traders make their wealth from the margins in moving things from areas of low value to high value (and vice versa). They are masters of timing and trends.

I used to have a client, Steve, who is a designer of big hotel complexes. We both have an interest in modern art and in Trader profile Flow he gave me a tip for buying art. Steve's focus was not on the artwork itself, but rather on the elements of timing that could affect the transaction. He recommended buying the work of a particular artist who was popular but very elderly in the knowledge that the value of an artist's work tends to increase posthumously. Although this strategy may at first sound a little insensitive, it is a common and accepted approach for investment in the art world.

Sitting midway between being system- and people-driven, the Trader can tend toward one of two strategies: making money through analysing data and trends or negotiating with people to improve their margins. Traders do not necessarily have to be stock-market traders. I find lots of Traders working in busy restaurants and bars, or on market stalls. As administrators they are some of the most efficient and productive profiles you will find.

Trader profiles are naturally attracted to high-pressure, high-turnover environments. Casualty wards in hospitals are where the doctors with Trader profiles are found. Under pressure they prioritize well and work quickly to ensure the flow of casualties under their care. They are incredibly efficient within a set of defined working parameters, which is something to bear in mind if you have a Trader profile on your team. Give them the structure and they'll fly! They are very much the 'doers' and 'implementers' of the Money Genius matrix.

They also make great carers. Again, they excel at doing repetitive tasks such as feeding and bathing patients, day in and day out. Nurses are often Trader profiles, and as Traders sit midway between systems and people, they tend to like the human interaction that nursing gives them.

Traders are also amazing humanitarians. Gandhi and Mandela are both Trader profiles. Jim Rogers, a well-known US market trader, is a stunning example, as he sees his trading income as a means of supporting his humanitarian efforts. People of the Trading profile are often disheartened by the almost cold term 'Trader' because this is by no means all they are. An alternative name for them would be 'Servers', taking in to account their heartfelt desire to serve their fellow humans.

In some ways they make good coaches as they are very grounded, caring, and insightful about what is happening in the moment for a person, but they aren't interested in the bigger picture. They give support where their patients and clients are, but don't tend to push them to move out of this dependence.

Having said that, there are a large percentage of traders who have an hour-glass shaped profile – heavy both on the Trader and the Creator. One of my stock-trading friends has this profile. He recently started his own coaching and trading business for advanced traders. His Creator side comes out in having the drive to start up his own enterprise on his own terms, with his own idea and models. But his Trader profile is very evident when he's trading, even down to the monotony in his voice, and his cool, calm demeanor when markets are moving fast and huge positions are on the line.

Traders are the opposite of Creators in that they are not concerned with the big picture or vision. They just like to get on with the task in hand. However, these hour-glass profile types of the Trader–Creator combination seem to have the same vision and big-picture thinking as the Creator. This is a good combination for starting a business, because the Creator part of the personality has the vision, and the Trader is good at implementation (the very thing Creators often struggle with initially).

Great at getting things done, Traders are most stressed when they have nothing to do. This means that if you manage a Trader, the trick to keep them in Flow and happy is to give them lots of work to do. (Do this to a Lord, an Accumulator, or a Mechanic and they quickly slip into overwhelm! Do it with a Star, a Creator, or a Mechanic and they will get distracted.)

To raise your effectiveness as a Trader profile the things you need to do are:

1. Find a system that already works and work with it.

2. 'Bake your own cake,' as my first trading coach used to tell me. This means implementing a 'recipe' or a system that you know works, then making

adjustments and tweaks based on what you notice is effective in order to maximize your margins.

3. Generate maximum value in whatever task you undertake by making sure you can control both sides of the transaction – the price and the timing of the purchase. For example, you need to have control of both the sourcing and the sale of the goods, so you never have a surplus or a deficit that is going to cost you margins.

4. Gather a team around you to do all the things that take you away from the transaction or trade, or being in front of the customer. For example, if you're managing operations, you shouldn't be doing book-keeping. If you're selling advertising space, you shouldn't be involved in getting the artwork done. If you're trading the markets, you shouldn't be spending time meeting potential investors – that would be the job of a Deal Maker on your team.

5. Make your money from the spread – the difference between what you buy and sell at. Learning how to manage cash flow is key to this.

Accumulator (collector, gatherer, hoarder)

'Collecting appreciating assets'

Whilst Traders make money from the flow of goods or services and the margins, Accumulators buy and hold on a rising tide. Whereas Stars are avid spenders, their opposite on the profile matrix, Accumulators, are keen savers. Their value lies in their ability to accumulate assets and then generate cash flow out of them.

At low energies they are known for hoarding, which seriously messes with the feng shui aspects of their space and their flow of cash. Clearing out is a good strategy for them to embrace when clutter seems to impose on any area of their lives.

Accumulators need to learn what to hang on to and what to discard. In holding on to the highest appreciating assets and cutting loose the dead wood, they can easily streamline their portfolios. Those with a good focus and leaning toward having a secondary Lord profile can get into the detail and do this most effectively.

Also at low energies they often fail through not cutting the rest of the team in on the deal and giving them enough incentive. Furthermore, whilst they thrive on detail, unless they understand what it means to their finances or to a business, they can be as adept as a Star at letting money run through their fingers. What's more, under pressure they are very slow to act, and are easily paralyzed from taking the necessary action because the odds and the circumstances seem overwhelming. When it's all going wrong they need good sound advice from a grounded source they can trust to get them out of a fix.

Accumulators need to have advocates to network on their behalf when building, as they are not good at sniffing out the deals for themselves because this is a people-facing task. This is where they need to team up with a Supporter or a Deal Maker profile.

The key thing for an Accumulator is to develop a definition of what they'd like to accumulate and then stick to it. Often they procrastinate and don't get into a deal simply because they haven't defined what a good deal looks like. They can alleviate this problem once they have a few deals under their belt, as they then have a real benchmark to compare future investments against.

Accumulators are great to have on a team because they make sure that everything is in order and done on time. They are phenomenal at research and gathering data. The difficulty is in getting them to summarize the detail in a meaningful way and draw valuable conclusions – a skill they need to develop in order to harness their immense value.

Warren Buffett is an Accumulator profile. He was once purported to have never sold a stock in his life and this underpins his general strategy: only buying into good companies that he would be happy to own long-term, and then holding onto their stock indefinitely.

To raise your effectiveness as an Accumulator profile, the things you need to do are:

1. Accumulate appreciating assets, be they companies, properties, or any other kind.

2. Decide on the niche you want to invest your time and skills in. Get specific with this and specialize as much as possible. There is a lot to learn in any area where you can accumulate assets. The better you define your area of expertise, the greater your chance of mastering that niche and strategy.

3. Know what a good deal for you looks like. That way, when a Deal Maker approaches you with a deal you can quickly evaluate whether it lies within your Flow and remit. For instance, if you're investing in companies, you may decide that your criteria are to select only companies that have been trading for two years or more, have more than four members of staff, and are in the computing sector. If you are in property, you may decide that you only want to buy and hold residential properties with more than three bedrooms, in a specific area that you are already familiar with. This cuts down massively on risk as you know the background information to the deal already and it saves huge amounts of time on research.

4. Find a Star, a Supporter, or even a Deal Maker to network on your behalf. You need someone to bring you the opportunities and to connect you with the finance.

5. Cultivate a stunning performance history on your portfolio. This is your biggest asset when securing finance. Investors like to see that you generate results and that their money is in safe hands. As an Accumulator profile, your hands are some of the safest around. Make sure you can demonstrate this.

6. Generate cash (for costs and living) from refinancing appreciating assets or issuing tradable shares in the assets.

Lord (researcher, analyser, maven)

'Controlling cash-generating assets'

Lords generate their wealth through controlling assets. They don't necessarily need to own the asset, just to control it – as in lease-option strategies, for instance. In fact, the motto of the Lord profile is to 'Own nothing, control everything.'

Great with detail, Lords are renowned for their thrift. These are the guys in a business who will sit down with the Creator profile and demonstrate how they've done some analysis on the phone lines a business is using and instead of needing four lines, they actually only need three, which will save the business a whopping $36 (£24) per month! They are indeed great analysts.

Lords are needed in an enterprise once there is something to manage. It's no good enrolling them at the dynamic initial stages when everything is in flux, unless you perhaps need to consult them on complicated laws and rules, for example. As you will see when we talk about cycles and the *I Ching* in the next chapter, their energy in a start-up or sapling environment stifles things as they try to pin details and processes down too soon in a project's development.

The other thing Lord profiles need to bear in mind is that micromanagement is a great strategy for cash flow, but not so great with people. The Gerber philosophy of measure and monitor everything is great in principle, but have you ever tried micromanaging a salesperson? Not a strategy I would recommend, as you never get the best out of them that way. As we have already seen, salespeople tend to be on the people side of the profile matrix – and whilst focus is always a good idea, micromanagement is a bridge too far and stunts their productivity massively.

And this brings us back to what we were originally saying – by understanding the profiles involved in your projects, you will start to see where they can be left to run under their own steam and take on more and more responsibility. The amount of management needed ultimately decreases as each person develops into their Flow and works more in the power of their own Money Genius.

Lords are invaluable to an established team or business. They're great at trimming the fat and crunching the numbers to make sure you're as efficient as you can be; superb with detail; and fantastic with research.

A Lord friend of mine has just completed a copywriting job in which she was commissioned to write 250 articles on astrology! This is where she flicked into researcher– maven (expert) mode, becoming avidly engrossed in all the possible articles she could generate interesting and useful content from. A Star would have stopped at two; a Creator would have sketched out the big picture for the series in bold brush strokes; a Deal Maker would have found someone else to write them; and an Accumulator would have gone to the library, done the research, taken a stash of books home, and then started searching Amazon for more books. They would still be thinking about getting started on it! The Lord profile will do the task set from beginning to end, though keeping to deadlines is often an issue as perfectionism has a tendency to creep in.

If you are a Lord profile, deadlines are your friend. Set yourself (realistic) timescales and then keep to them. They will help you overcome procrastination and get completion on many more things than you would without them. At higher energies, on larger scales, Lords have an excellent eye for dominating an entire industry. One example of this would be the brewing industry in the UK.

The breweries are the factories that produce beer. However, they own a large percentage of public houses (pubs) through which they sell the beers and other alcoholic drinks that they manufacture. They also own a number of the farms that produce the hops that supply them. In this way, they own every step of the process from growing the hops, to producing the beverage, to selling it retail.

They then also sell their beer wholesale to supermarkets, often simply putting it in different packaging so the supermarkets can sell it as their own brand. This is a classic Lord business, where each step along a process is controlled by the single entity in a vertical arrangement (as opposed to horizontal, which would mean that there was only one brewery that owned all the factories).

In a similar way, Andrew Carnegie, the industrialist and philanthropist, originally invested in railcars and railroads, and later moved into investing in iron, the raw material required for the rail industry. He was heavily involved in developing and rationalizing the process of producing steel from iron. It was here that he amassed his huge wealth, and this again shows us how the Lord profile has a tendency toward vertical acquisition to secure control of the assets. The rail industry was clearly completely dependent on the output of the iron industry when Carnegie effectively took control of the industry toll booth. Anyone wishing to build railways and bridges needed to pay him for the steel they required.

To raise your effectiveness as a Lord profile the things you need to do are:

1. Focus on selecting and financing assets that will generate the cash you want. To create more income, find more assets to give you that cash flow.

2. Stick to the same niche when expanding your portfolio, as this will keep down the cost of resources, research time, and spread of expertise.

3. Find a Supporter or Deal Maker to bring you a network of resources and deals. Fight the tendency to isolate yourself now and again and connect with these players in your team. They are your link to your wealth.

4. Use the model of owning the toll booth, rather than the bridge and the river. For example, Google Adwords owns the flow of information and traffic (not the content or the businesses) that use adwords. They take a toll for directing traffic flow to the businesses. This is a Lord profile strategy.

5. You already own the cash flow by definition of the strategy, but you need to be able to control what you charge for your deliverables, and its worth paying attention to things like the interest you're paying on financing deals and what you're paying for your assets. Remember, you're squeezing cash

out of an asset you don't necessarily own. Explore all possibilities to do this. This is where you will naturally excel.

Mechanic (engineer, tinkerer, improver)

'Creating a better system'

The phrase 'creating a better system' presupposes you have a system set up already. You cannot rely on Mechanics to get started from nothing – it will never happen and it is a painful process. Mechanics are great at working on processes and projects that already exist, but not so good at pulling ideas from the ether and getting them physically started. However, give them specific tasks and they're away. The tasks that suit them most are tinkering with something that already exists or something with a framework.

Mechanics, I've found, are very good at homing in on the detail and doing things like writing articles and books. They're brilliant at churning out detail for blogs and anything that you can take in small, methodical chunks. They also make fantastic copywriters if writing is one of their skills. They have the patience to figure out which phrases work, and then to implement them, test them, rewrite them, and then test again. They are amazing at understanding systems and improving them. See the pattern? They can take something that exists and always make it better. They are incredibly process-driven.

You may be interested in how Sam Walton built up Walmart. He started off with just a single store, which soon turned into several. But he became obsessed with noticing what worked and what didn't. It's been said that he used to spend more time in his competitors' stores than in his own, because what he would be looking for would be the next idea that he could implement in his business to build up profits and increase the value he could distribute to his customers. He was always looking to improve the existing system by making tweaks and changes, and adding in new lines that no one else had thought of. All of a sudden clothing was being sold through his distribution system, added in as another commodity that people could buy, since they were there in the supermarket anyway. He became a master of distribution.

And when Mechanic profiles find a process to whatever it is they're doing, they become unstoppable! For example, one colleague, years ago, found an eBook strategy someone else was doing. He then researched a few specific (profitable) niches and wrote his own eBooks for them. He implemented the original strategy, made changes to make it more effective, such as setting up a series of 50 auto-responder messages, drove some traffic, and watched money come into his shopping cart account. What made him a masterful Mechanic profile was that he then tweaked his own process to make it even better and watched the conversion rates increase.

The high flyers with this profile systemize this process, package it up, and then use their system to sell the original system, making more money from this last step than they made in the entire run-up to it! Have you ever wondered why the business of teaching internet marketing is so competitive? This is why. These Super-Mechanic profiles build up from grass roots, and sell or franchise their process, and then package the selling of the process before selling that. Each time they deal with larger abstractions but also greater value packages. Genius!

If you are a Mechanic profile trying to start up on your own, consider working with someone else on the other side of the square, preferably someone who is already up and running. Plug in to their Flow. You will increase their Flow massively by making crucial changes to their process, allowing them to make even more money. Before you implement the changes though, be sure to agree on how much of the uplift you are entitled to, so that you, too, benefit from the increased revenue.

Many Mechanics I know still haven't started their projects because they are still trying to find the traction to get going. In these instances they haven't taken sufficient action in one direction because they are still trying to figure out which route to take. The best thing for a Mechanic in this situation is to pick a route and go with it. Get some results. Then course-correct along the way.

To raise your effectiveness as a Mechanic profile the things you need to do are:

1. Align yourself with people who are already running a business or have a product, and help them to increase distribution or implement the systems to increase their volume and automate as far as reasonable.

2. Make your systems idiot-proof and scalable.

3. Focus on testing, refining, measuring performance, and improving the system.

4. Ensure you have agreements or contracts in place allowing you to benefit directly from the improvements in the system that will increase the bottom line.

Most people with Mechanic profiles I have worked with have excelled at systemizing processes already existing in some form in businesses that are already trading. The kinds of things they improve are distribution, client acquisition, delivery of the product or service, and the franchising of the final system into other similar businesses. This is a real example of finding someone or an enterprise in Flow, and then multiplying that Flow by adding your own unique type of value or Flow to it.

So you see, each of the eight Money Genius profiles has a different energy about it, and they offer very different strategies to create wealth.

Knowing where your strengths are and doing what you need to do are two different things. Sometimes we know what we *should* be doing, but we have so much resistance and fear around doing it that we just don't take the necessary steps to generate the results we seek. When this happens the best thing to do is go back to the releasing chart and work through an exercise on the specific issue. So, say for example you are a Star profile, and you know you need to be giving more talks but you have a fear of public speaking, then you need to do some releasing around speaking on stage.

Knowing not just what to do but how to go about it can sometimes be confusing. Where do you start? Who can you ask? What should you do? How much should you spend/invest in a given task? Again, letting go of thoughts around a desired outcome is the perfect way to clear up that confusion and get to a place where you just know what to do. Do the exercises again and again and you can't fail.

Now you'll probably be thinking that if you only do the things you enjoy, how does everything else in your business get done? For example, if you're a Supporter profile and love putting on events and networking with people, who will sit down and do your tax returns, or look after your website, or send out your invoices? This is an excellent question, and it brings us deeper into the heart of the idea of embracing your Money Genius.

As we've already mentioned, just because you don't like doing a task, doesn't mean that it won't be within someone else's Flow. Indeed, the very fact that it *isn't* within your Flow, means that it *will be* within the Flow of someone else in the wealth matrix. The thing to do is identify which profile would excel at that task, and then attract the correct person for that role.

From there we can work on bringing together small teams of people with different profiles in order to achieve an energetic balance for the project or enterprise, depending on the type of energy it requires. For example, running around and getting investor support for a new business venture needs a fresh, new energy. At the early stages of a business things are crisp and unformed. Individuals need to be dynamic and flexible. This is not an arena for someone who is rigid and unyielding. A Lord or an Accumulator profile in the core launch team would very quickly stifle any blaze created by the necessary Creator, Star, or Supporter profiles.

Points to Remember

- Each person primarily fits one profile

- The key is to master the game of your profile

- Let go of doing things that fall outside the things your profile excels at

- Competence and Flow are two different things – always choose Flow, even if you can do something that isn't in your profile. This is how you achieve mastery.

In the next chapter we will discuss specifically how to attract the right people with the necessary Money Genius profiles.

Chapter 6
Key 4: Building Teams with Mojo

You've found where your own Money Genius is and now you're making changes. Great job!

But the next thing you have to do rather quickly in order to keep your business operating is to plug the gaps that are left when you stop doing the things that *you* personally shouldn't be doing. After all, if you're a Deal Maker and you have decided that putting products in the post really is stopping you from making the great deals that put the money on the bottom line, you're still going to have to get those products out somehow. For example, if you're a Star profile and you're spending all your time presenting to prospects or talking to journalists about your business, how are you going to submit your tax returns, or even make sure that the products you sell go out to your customers?

This is the fourth key – where your entrepreneurial team comes into play to multiply your Money Mojo! This key will mean that you can categorically always have your Mojo flowing, without having to force yourself to do things you're not naturally good at. And of course, the more time you spend in your Mojo, the better you become. The better you become, the more you will set yourself apart from your competition. The better you set yourself apart, the more business you will attract and the higher the income you will command, thus allowing you to outsource even more of what you're not naturally good at.

Now, if you're not already outsourcing, I know what you're thinking, because it's the same thing everyone says. You're wondering how you can afford to employ someone to do the things you don't like doing. I will soon reveal precisely how you can 'afford' to bring other people on board. But before we talk about that, let's just touch on what it is costing you *not* to have other people doing the things that are not in your Flow.

Let's stick with the example of a Star profile trying to do their book-keeping. Since this is a task not naturally in their Flow, it is never going to be something they are great at – even if they are as smart as a rocket scientist. They're always going to be putting it off and hemorrhaging energy into that task, which distracts them from excelling at the things they are amazing at. In this way it keeps them moving backward as it's a constant drain on their energy, their time (just tot up the amount of time you spend putting something off), and on their brain function (think about the number of useless thoughts that a non-Flow task takes up over a period of time). It's also going to be eroding their self-esteem – simply because it's something that doesn't make them feel great about themselves. They're likely to be constantly stressing about it, under the surface of their psyche, trying to mentally blackmail themselves to get the task done. Not very productive or profitable, is it?

Now, let's consider the converse. Say they outsource the book-keeping somehow. Say they don't ever have to worry about keeping on top of it again. Now they no longer have the guilt or the mental distraction. All the time they were previously spending either doing the book-keeping or thinking about it is immediately freed up. They can now spend this new free time and mental and emotional energy doing what they are wired to be doing – for example, delivering training sessions, sales presentations, or whatever else fits with their core talents as a Star profile in their business.

So, right now, have a think about all the things you force yourself to do. Think of those things that, if you had a magic wand, you'd quite happily allow someone else to do for you. You can list them in the first column in the table below.

Task	Number of hours	Cost to your business by doing them yourself	Cost of outsourcing to someone else

Now what if you had the cash to throw at these tasks, so that someone else would do them for you? You have probably realized already that this would give you massive returns very quickly, just in freeing you up to do the things that you should be doing. The very act of giving these tasks to someone else will quickly bring in much more cash.

But sometimes people find themselves in a 'cash trap': they haven't got time to step up to the next level in their business to generate more cash, because they're too busy doing the things they should really be giving someone else to do. Sometimes it's a matter of trusting first and allowing yourself the time to step up this new delegation, so that you're in a situation where you *can* afford it.

Another way of looking at this is to ask yourself what it is costing you in real cash terms to do those tasks yourself. The way you calculate this is by estimating, for each of the tasks listed above, how much time you're spending doing or procrastinating over them in a month.

Then, if you don't already know it, work out your hourly rate by taking the total amount of money you make in a month and dividing it by the number of hours you spend doing things that actually pull money into the business. Multiply your hourly rate by the number of hours you spend on each of the tasks you could delegate, and then decide if you could outsource it for less. You'll be surprised how often people find a motivation to do so, after doing this exercise. Sure, it's not cut and dried, but it gives you an indication of what you are missing out on.

Then fill out the remaining columns in the table to help you find out the figures for each task. And remember, it's not as if you have to pay people full-time salaries to do what you need. If you need tweaks done to your website, or banners redesigning, or book-keeping doing, it's easy to find people with the skills you need who won't charge you a fortune for their time. Here are a few suggestions:

1. Super teens: Teenagers are generally proficient in social media and computer-based technical tasks. Find one (maybe a relative or the son or daughter of a friend) and ask them to help you. Depending on the relationship, you may want to offer them an hourly rate or something of value in exchange. (I've known teenagers who would become incredibly resourceful when certain concert tickets were within their grasp!)

2. Students and stay-at-home mums: They can do an incredible job on all your administration tasks. In turn, this gives them the confidence to increase their skills, confidence, and income.

3. Skill swaps: Get creative with people you know and meet networking. If someone has a talent you could really use in your business, offer them your Money Mojo skills in return for their help. Be careful not to devalue your own products or services, though. Remember in Chapter 2 we talked about increasing the value we place on ourselves and our self-esteem? It's important to maintain this new self-esteem all the way through the process of generating more wealth. Don't compromise now!

4. The internet: This can be a great place to post and answer adverts for the skills you need. But make

sure they are packaged as small, easily defined tasks. Though you may find a rare gem, remember that a lot of these adverts are placed and answered at no cost and if the person who responds doesn't value the opportunity you're presenting, you may end up wasting your time. Also, always screen people carefully before you hand them tasks to perform.

5. Social media: Facebook is an incredible resource for finding people who are on the same wavelength. Some of my coaching clients have found me through Facebook, and I've met several joint-venture partners through contacts I already had on there. Spruce up your profile and be clear about what you do and what you are looking for. Then, make an effort to connect with people who might be in your niche.

6. Networking meetings, seminars, and workshops are great places to meet people and interact on a business level. Take the time to talk about what is important to them, and how you might help. Pay attention to what lights them up – they may have skills and Flow that complement yours.

7. Gold Nugget Suggestion: Find a Supporter profile in your niche! They will know many people who can assist you and will be able to suggest the most relevant people to approach. They will also have business relationships that allow them to tap out a friendly email introduction, thus making the other person more receptive to what you have to say.

*It's not about being able to afford it, but more about
how to attract people who are also in their money Flow,
who are drawn to your enterprise and want
to contribute.*

Action and Attracting Resources

Until we've mastered taking action and lifted our frequency high enough, we're never going to have enough energy or momentum to manifest the reality we desire in this dense, physical world. This inertia is great when we're in danger of manifesting damaging things through our stored negativity. It has served us well. But you will notice more and more, as you release layers of emotions and thoughts, that you become lighter and lighter. Your frequency will naturally increase and you will manifest things in your thoughts much more quickly.

Eventually, we reach a point where we are energetically high and clear enough to be able to make things happen all the time in the physical world. But before we can reach that level of consciousness, we still need to take some form of action in order to move forward. It's like saying to the Universe, and indeed those around us, that this is the direction we're heading in. This is where our energy is. This is what we are committed to. We spell it out by our actions.

Once you start moving in this way, you gather momentum. You see some success, and you become even more enthused about the path you are taking. What's more, others see that you are doing what you said you would do. They see you're making waves and they have an unconscious desire to tap in to your Flow. This is an excellent time to start gathering like-minded, progressive people around you to help you. The thing to do here is to engage with people who have the drive to move in a similar direction, and who also complement your profile.

Attracting Resources

So what do you do when you don't have the resources to employ someone? First, you need to decide which profile you need on your team; what skills they should have; which tasks need doing; which tasks the profile can help you with; and what your perfect team member will be like.

The best thing to do next is an emotional releasing exercise (see pages 58–71) around your ideal person simply showing up. Some of the things you might want to focus on will probably include:

- Accepting the idea of having someone else come on board

- Agreeing that you will share your business decisions with another person

- Believing it is possible for the right person just to show up

- Providing something in return for them – for example, payment or a skill exchange

- Coming to terms with the fact they will be an unknown quantity

And I'm sure you can think of other things to go on the list.

Often the arrival of a competent person can bring up lots of feelings of inadequacy and a need for security, simply because deep down you feel they might show you up and/or your business might suddenly become too successful for you to cope with within your comfort zone. Whatever feelings emerge, know that in letting go you have the tools to deal with them.

So now why not go ahead and think of any resistance you might have to attracting the right team around you and jot them down below?

1. _____

2. _____

3. _____

4. _____

5. _____

6. _____

You can then put these thoughts into the table below as we did in Chapter 3 (see page 67), and then let go of each thought one by one. As well as filling out the resistance (lower) part of the table, it is also well worthwhile to let go of the reasons why you'd like this new team member around. As we have already discussed, it is also the wanting that pushes the outcome away as well.

With ease and grace I allow myself to have a capable and productive member in my team.		
Reasons I want it	**Wanting love, wanting control, wanting security?**	**Let it go?**
Will free up my time		
Will make me more money ultimately		
Resistance to having it	**Wanting love, wanting control, wanting security?**	**Let it go?**
I can't afford it yet		
They will take time to train up		
It's quicker to do it myself		

When you've cleared out both sides of this outcome of having one or more new team members on board, you will then be much freer to allow the perfect team to find their way to you.

There are then some other factors to consider when you start bringing others into your vision.

The Mistakes People Make with a Team

1. Lack of trust: not giving team members the freedom they need. We need to let go and trust their ability and passion for what they do to work in the best interests of the project. Give them ownership.

2. Lack of team Flow: If one person is out of Flow, can the team be in Flow? Of course not! If there are frictions, don't 'manage' them or you'll always be managing them. Whatever the problem is, sort it out.

3. Lack of complementary energy frequency: Only consider people who are on the same energetic frequency as you are. Don't assume you will ever change someone. If a person is downbeat and negative, you are not going to turn them into a productive go-getter – you will waste lots of valuable time and energy trying. Besides, it not anyone's place to impose on someone else their own value system or beliefs about how they should or shouldn't be. Find people who resonate with you and what you stand for. If you're attracting people with low energy, who seem to bring your team down, then it's an opportunity to look in the mirror and check whether they are reflecting a disowned part of yourself. Dig deep. It'll feel wonderful to let go of whatever comes up.

People are attracted to momentum. And certainty. You will never have a problem attracting great people if you can deliver on both these things.

Who Do I Need in My Team?

So far we've talked about skills that can be outsourced. However, there may be aspects of your business that require someone who sings from the same hymn sheet, has skills that complement yours, and who is prepared to join you for the longer term.

First and foremost, the thing to do here is to really focus on what the purpose of your business is. Hone it so that it 'sings' to you. Make sure it compels you, so that you are completely sold on the idea, and then go out and win over other people with the vision of what you want to achieve and why. Make your vision bigger than you are – it will move you, and those around you, to do things you would normally be too scared to do.

Through talking with other people you will find that certain individuals are naturally drawn to your business. They'll want to be involved, just because it lights them up and speaks to their inner desires. They'll also see that you're using your Money Mojo to the full, and they'll want to plug in and join the party.

At this point, if they fit with your vision, you'll want to get them profiled to see if they suit the dynamics of your business and really have the missing Mojo to contribute – after all, it would be no good bringing someone on board who has the same Money Genius Type as you, because collectively you won't have the specific energy types required to evolve the business.

So, there are a couple of ways of deciding which profile to bring on board next.

The Tripod System: Which Profile Next?

The tripod system refers to the idea that your initial core team should be made up of individuals whose matrix profiles are as far apart from each other as possible. This ensures that the smallest number of people offers the best range of skills and energy types to draw from. Firstly, let's remind ourselves of the eight Wealth Profiles:

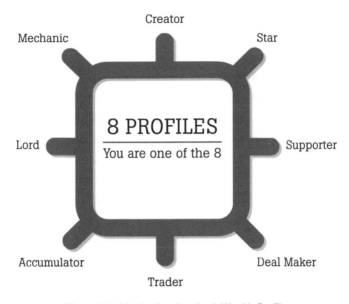

Figure 6.1: Matrix showing the 8 Wealth Profiles

Generally, the rough and ready way to determine this would be to count two profiles clockwise around the matrix from your own profile, and the third profile you come to is team member number two. Then go back to your profile and count two profiles anti-clockwise, and your third team member is that profile. This is an approximate way to work it out, but there are specific suggested profile combinations – a discussion of which is a little beyond the scope of this book. So, working with the tripod method, if you were a Creator profile your number two would be a Deal Maker and the next new team member would be an Accumulator.

The other approach would be to work out which profile you need in your business, and then set an intention to find such a person, so that they find you when you go out talking to people.

Let me tell you about David, by way of example, and you'll understand how this works. David is a Mechanic profile and he was desperately running around doing site surveys and quoting for jobs in his construction business. Not only was this *out* of his Flow but it meant he never had time to do what was *in* his Flow – to tweak the systems of the business to make them more effective and deliver an even better service to his clients – the very thing that set him apart from the competition.

Immediately it was obvious that he not only needed more people on his team, but he needed specific profiles for certain jobs. First off, he needed someone in the office to help him organize things whilst he was out on the road. This was an internal project management role. It would involve coordinating contractors, materials, and fielding client queries and requests, as well as supporting David whilst he was out of the office. He needed a Supporter profile.

Then, very quickly, it became evident that he could, and should, offload the site surveys and running the jobs on site himself. He had done enough of them to be able to refine the system he had devised and was just getting bored and frustrated with the same routine every day. He needed a Trader profile to take over this kind of high-churn project management. Remember, Trader profiles are excellent at getting lots done, fast. In fact, they're brilliant at dealing with the here and now, hands-on problem solving, and are more stressed when they have nothing to do.

Now, there is also a lot of paperwork involved in construction – a lot of forms to fill in, regulations to conform to, and boxes that need ticking. This would be the perfect task for a back-office Lord profile.

Within a few months of deciding his strategy and using the other keys I'm about to share with you, David was able to recruit exactly the right profiles into each of the roles we discussed, which resulted in massive shifts in the business. In doing this, he created a team of individuals each working to their own personal Money Genius profile, doing what came naturally and easily to them and what kept them doing only the things that they loved doing. Together they turned the business around from being massively in debt and just about to fold to a very profitable business, which is now on track and hitting targets month after month.

So you see how important it is to have a team of people, all pulling in the same direction, with each person playing to their natural strengths in everything they do for the business? This makes for a highly productive, happy, and inevitably successful team, from the beginning.

The other point to note is that David did well to ensure he had a spread of profiles on board, so that there was a balance of energies for doing what needed to be done, particularly in the transition period when they were making lots of changes to how they ran the business and who did what. The change he made to his recruitment strategy was particularly useful, as in the past he had had a tendency to bring on board only people who were just like him – people he felt comfortable around and could easily relate to.

Often when we start working more closely with people on the other side of the profile matrix from us, we find it uncomfortable simply because they have a different personality. For example, Supporters, who are very people-orientated, would be flabbergasted to show up at an event only to see a Lord profile reading a newspaper in the middle of a packed room! These are the kinds of things we have to get over, though, in order to respect and work effectively with people who value things differently. A Lord profile may simply value the information they are reading in a newspaper more than the potential connections they could gain from networking in a room full of strangers. And the ability to focus when so much is going on around you can be a powerful strength – for instance, when you need to sift through a lot of information in the workplace and there are other distractions around you.

Who *Don't* I Need in My Team?

When you're creating a team, the thing *not* to do is to bring on board people who have the same profile as you. I've seen a number of service-based businesses where two or three of the main directors have all been Creator profiles. Sometimes it works for a little while, but ultimately it either remains an ongoing struggle or ends in tears. To state the obvious: Creator profiles are creative. They're streaming with ideas and insights. Even just one Creator in a team is enough to send most other team members' heads spinning when they get into their creative Flow.

Creators have so many visions for their businesses and so many ideas to implement that having just one channel produces enough for any business to harness and use effectively. And even then, the most effective Creators edit and veto a lot of their ideas before they bring them to the team to consider. Now, when you have two or more Creators in one business the results can be particularly destructive, as each wants to have their own idea implemented and feels that their way is the best. If everything remains amicable the business becomes at best a mish-mash of identities – a design by committee. The other problem is that there aren't enough team players to get anything done. You have two or three Creators at the helm of the ship, shouting out directions, but not enough sailors to actually carry out the changes!

If this is your situation, think really carefully about what you expect from your business. You may want to ask yourself the following questions:

- Do you want it to remain at this level?

- Do you want to step things up a level and for things to change somehow?

- Are you making enough money playing at this level to sustain you all?

- Are the other Creator profiles in agreement with how it should change?

- What is the potential cost of continuing in this format if everyone isn't in agreement with how it should evolve?

- What's stopping you from going out on your own?

Now, you may think that this is a potential risk for any partnership – but the thing to bear in mind is that most other profiles are more amenable to being led and guided to success. Creators just need to create – and you wouldn't have deprived Picasso of his paintbrush, would you?

Let's now move on to another group of profiles who shouldn't work together.

A Warning to Creator, Star, and Supporter Profiles

These three profiles love working together... initially. But as there is no balance for their energies, they soon find they want to keep creating in different directions and they have little traction for doing the implementation required in any project. If you're in this situation, be honest with yourself as to whether or not you are making any solid progress. It may be an idea to each go your separate ways and readdress what you really want to achieve. Then, when it comes to the point where you need a team, stick to recruiting people on the basis of their skills and their profiles, to make sure you get the right balance of energy around the matrix. This will prevent you from getting stuck the next time around.

If you don't know the profiles of your team members, just work through the steps at www.wireyourselfforwealth. com to find out and get your team in Flow.

When Recruiting, Why Do We Go Clockwise Round the Matrix First?

As we've already mentioned, each profile has a different skill set, but each also has a different energy. In fact, they have the energies that take on the characteristics of the seasons. Starting at the top, the Creator has the energy of spring: 'springing' with fresh new ideas. Moving round clockwise to the Supporter profile, we see a summer energy – the idea has developed into a blaze of chatter that the Supporter can put through their network to their employees or acquaintances, who can glean mutual benefit. By the time the idea gets round to where the Trader profile comes into play, it's become a commodity – an autumn energy. Then, before the concept returns to spring, it goes through winter, where the Lord profile is able to cut out the dead wood and refine it to make it more profitable, before it becomes reborn under another guise.

An example of this process would be the development of the iPhone, which gained legendary status before it was even launched. Everyone was talking about the iPhone, it was discussed endlessly on internet forums, and there was a general buzz throughout the spring and summer of its existence, every time a little bit of information was leaked or announced about its features and its much-anticipated arrival. The concept was viral in the networks featuring gadgets long before it ever came on sale. By the time it became a commodity we could buy in the shops, it was already a known sensation.

Then the iPhone was redeveloped, after the mass market had used it and fed back the improvements that could be made, and it moved through from autumn to winter. In the winter period we saw the cost come down dramatically, and it became available on most mobile networks. In other words the Flow of the product was multiplied through more distribution channels. (Recall how the Lord profiles 'trim the fat,' and simplify things as much as possible to make them multipliable; and Mechanics 'reinvent from what already exists.' Do you see the pattern emerging?) And then what was created out of its wake? Yes, a new iPhone, with better battery-life, more apps, a more versatile and flexible operating system, and so on: the iPhone 4.

You can track the same evolution for the iPad, which runs from a very similar user interface and concept. What about the iPad 2? And yet Apple say, 'If you ask us, we'd say this is only the beginning...'

Your team should evolve in the same way. It generally starts with a Creator profile. Often, but not always, a Creator spawns the idea that develops into a new business. The natural evolution then is to bring on board someone who can sell the idea to investors and customers. This is a Star-profile task. That's not to say a Creator couldn't pitch their idea to potential investors. It's just that this kind of thing comes more naturally to a Star, leaving the Creator to hone the idea and work behind the scenes to get it ready for market. Stars are also in tune with their audience and are able to simplify the concepts for mass consumption. Creators can get stuck in both the big picture and the detail of their product, and most investors are quite specific about what they want to know concerning an opportunity.

The Star energy then requires the skills of a Supporter, someone with a network relevant to the project, who can take the concept out into the marketplace and generate feedback and initial sales and investments. When I think of this stage, I consider how Stars can warm up cold contacts from a stage, and how Supporters then use their warm network of targeted contacts.

It is this move toward leveraging the value from a network that allows the project to flourish. At the first stage, the Creator profile probably doesn't know a huge number of people who will be very useful. However, if you multiply his idea by the possibilities and knowledge in all of the Supporter's contacts, you very quickly have a core group of valuable people able to bring the idea to market.

Had the Creator gone the other way round the matrix, he would have brought on board a Mechanic profile, who would then be intent on making the product/concept better and better, without ever taking it to market. The project would have failed at the first hurdle and never brought in any money to sustain the growth of the business.

By the same token, bringing winter profiles (Mechanics, Lords, and Accumulators) into the business too early will cut the growth and development too soon. The business will become stunted and will probably fail if it is brought into the refining and fat-trimming stage before time.

Seasons in Economies

The seasons show up in teams, in projects, and in relationships. Even economies are subject to this cycle: local economies, global economies, specific markets, the UK property market – everything. Trader profiles are naturally attuned to the seasons in their particular niche and if they are to maximize their wealth, they also need to attune themselves to what their niche or market economy is doing, and work directly with that ebb and flow.

Understanding these seasons will help you maximize your collective Mojo, and appreciate where you are in your projects seasonally, so you know what you should be doing at each point – pushing forward or letting go – so you can benefit from the ebbs and flows in projects.

It's counterproductive to be pushing on and investing heavily in new marketing methods if your business is actually in an autumn phase, needing some grounded energy to make more trade. Focusing elsewhere will mean you miss the opportunities and deals happening there and then. If you can recognize where in the cycle your project is, you can harness the energy in much the same way as we can use tidal forces to generate electricity.

Pay attention to the ebb and flow, and work with it rather than against it. This will mean you can conserve resources on the ebbs and maximize on the flows. Plus it makes life much more relaxed and sustainable! Of course, there are cycles within cycles, but stepping back and appreciating this will certainly help you to make the most of the natural fluctuations in your business, the marketplace, and the economy.

Check List for Building an Entrepreneurial Team with Mojo

1. 'Know Thyself' – know your own profile and where your own Mojo is. Get yourself in Flow.

2. Have a compelling vision – when this is attractive enough, people will gravitate toward you.

3. Decide what your business needs in order to move up to the next level. What is stopping you from making more money right now? Write these things down. Which is the biggest hindrance on the list? This will be the one you get rid of.

4. Clear out any resistance or desire you have toward having a team around you, as per the grid earlier in this chapter (see page 146).

5. Work out which profile would be best suited to the task you have decided you need to outsource or give to your team.

6. Attract this profile to your cause (see the next chapter for techniques to increase your manifesting abilities). When you find people who you think may fit, work through the steps at www.wireyourselfforwealth.com to find out what their profile is. This will save you a lot of time and expense messing around with people who may not be suitable for your team.

7. Bear in mind your business will move through seasons – make sure the energies you have on your team don't stunt growth or cause growth to overextend the present level of business.

Points to Remember

- Gather other profiles around you to do the tasks that are off-profile for you

- You don't need to employ people, just partner, outsource, and profit-share

- To attract the right people have a vision bigger than you are. Show them the results you are already achieving – people are drawn to Flow that is already happening

- Release any emotional baggage you have around having or attracting a team

- People who are not like you can be your bridge to greater things

Next, we are going to explore the fifth key – how to boost your ability to get results.

Chapter 7
Key 5: Developing Your Ability to Get Results

In the last couple of chapters we have got to know our strengths. We have considered how to put a strong team together and how to get them working to their inner Money Genius type. Now it's time to look at how to make it all happen.

The first thing is to start doing more tasks and activities that are within your profile. Do the things that light you up and get you into Flow. Let that excitement to get going really take over and expand. Now although you probably agree with this, I expect you are thinking that in order to start doing more tasks and activities within your profile you first need more money, more time, a website, more clients, some new ideas, a logo, a system, an accountant... or whatever (you fill in the blanks).

This is where the fifth key to wiring yourself for wealth comes in. The fifth key is about using your natural Mojo to manifest the things you need or indeed the results you choose – as long as they are truly aligned with who you are and not some picture created out of ego, or even worse, what you *think* you should want.

Let me explain. The easiest way to manifest something is to choose the goals or things that deep down you really want, the goals and things you know will serve you. These will be the easiest to attain. They will also take less effort and energy – like pushing a rock downhill. And when these things materialize, you will feel fulfilled and satisfied.

However, if you try to manifest things to plug a gap in your life or because you want to compete with someone else's vision, not only will it take much more effort and energy, but you will probably feel disappointed with the end result when you achieve it. You'll then move straight on to the next thing in the belief that attaining this will make you feel more satisfied. In this second scenario you gain nothing and there is no growth.

However, if by contrast you start from a place of completion, where everything is already perfect and you don't need to 'get' anything in order to feel worthy, or to feel good about yourself, you are already coming from a place of power. Everything you create from this place is merely a manifestation on the canvas of your life. You unleash your innate creativity and are already fulfilled, so you have no attachment to what you create. From here you feel completely free to create what you like because you *can*. Do you feel the difference?

The other thing is that it is much easier to make something happen when you're doing it with the right intention and when the process lights you up. You've probably noticed this in your experience already. When you try to create an outcome solely because you need the money or security, you probably find it a lot tougher than when you do it just because you're inspired to. And besides, why use up your power to manifest things that take you away from doing what you love and living your true purpose? That's crazy, isn't it?

Alignment Check

So you may want to consider this next thing very seriously. If there is no correlation between what lights you up and your Vehicle of Value Conversion, now would be a good time to seriously consider if you're putting your efforts into the wrong thing. Remember, our aim is to get our Money Mojo going and aligned with what we really want. It's just not effective to align it with something that we feel we *have to* or *should* do. And don't worry for now about how to extract yourself from the current business, or job, or niche that you've been working in. We'll come to that later.

For now, just take a minute to allow your mind to wander over the possibilities of what would light you up and get you working day and night, just for the sheer joy of it.

So, with your higher purpose in mind, what are the things that you would like to create in your world? Have a think about this and then complete the exercise below.

....

EXERCISE: FOCUSING ON YOUR IDEAL LIFE

What would your world be like, on a day-to-day basis, if you could create it any way you choose?

1. Jot down your initial ideas. Then you may want to refer back to the exercise in Chapter 4 (see page 83), in which you noted down what came naturally to you and what you loved doing.

2. Now perhaps you'd like to consider what things, people, and experiences you need to attract to help you achieve your intention. Make a list – you can keep coming back to this to add to it, or decide to cross off those that are no longer relevant. This is a living list. (Over time, it will change, and if you hold in mind your inner purpose the list is more likely to focus in on this, rather than diverge to lots of potentially conflicting goals.)

3. So now that you know what you want to create in your world, and how you wish to experience those things, I'd like you to think of any obstacles to achieving the outcomes you've written down in Steps 1 and 2? Go ahead and jot those down, too.

Keep all this information together as you are going to need it when we learn how to remove the obstacles, below.

....

Assuming that emotional baggage is the cause of the obstacles you wrote down in the exercise above, I'd now like to show you how to release it, so that the obstacles no longer exist as either an excuse or a version of reality in your mind. In this way, the perceived obstacles will resolve themselves.

We need to release the baggage that is causing the obstacles emotionally and energetically from our systems. Remember, the obstacles are merely physical manifestations of the baggage we carry around.

So, say one obstacle is 'I can't attract money.' We're not going to worry about whether or not that thought is true – we don't need to. All we're interested in is finding any emotional baggage that it has attached to it, cleaning it off, and then discarding the statement as just another thought that passed through our mind.

You may recall the letting-go exercise we did in Chapter 3 (see page 56) as part of the second key. Our next process is similar, but instead of confining ourselves to what we perceive to be the reasons for resistance to our desired outcome, we're going to release any thoughts about the obstacle, so that we can start to realize the pictures we hold in our mind as reality are just a series of thoughts that are neither real nor unreal. They're just thoughts.

To help us do this we're going to change each 'obstacle' statement into a 'permission' statement.

Here are a couple of examples:

I can't attract money (OBSTACLE STATEMENT) becomes *I allow myself to have $15,000 (£10,000) in my account with ease and grace.* (PERMISSION STATEMENT).

I haven't got enough money to outsource my web design (OBSTACLE STATEMENT) becomes *I allow myself to outsource my web design with ease and grace.* (PERMISSION STATEMENT).

We then set about the task of weeding out any thoughts that come up in association with the new statement. It could be anything: *I'm not good enough*; *I can't afford it*; *I haven't got time*; *I'm too tired*; *I'm not sure it's the right thing to do right now*; and so on.

Whatever thought comes into your head about the new statement, go ahead and write it down in the first column.

New Goal Statement: I allow myself to...		
Thoughts about that statement	Is that wanting love, wanting control, or wanting security?	Could I let it go?

The next thing to do is recognize that thought as one of those three categories of 'want': wanting love, wanting control, or wanting security. Write the answer in the second column. Then you will want to let it go, using the three questions:

1. Whichever want it is, could I let it go?   Yes

2. If I could, would I?   Yes

3. When is a good time?   Now

And when you've let that want go, you can just tick it off in the third column.

So, go ahead and copy the grid down and turn each obstacle into a permission statement. Then knock out all the resistance to having that goal as reality. Keep going until you've turned each obstacle into an 'I allow myself' statement and cleared it out using the emotional releasing questions.

Take your time with this. It's worth putting in the effort to dig up whatever conscious and unconscious thoughts may occur to you. Even if something comes up that doesn't really hit a chord with you, or doesn't seem to have a whole lot of feeling attached to it, write it down and release it anyway. You may be surprised at what issues are lurking beneath it!

Once you're familiar with this exercise, you want to step up and work on the next level. So, assuming your inner Mojo is in alignment with your current business, you may want to do the above exercise again, focusing on the specific things you feel would be of great benefit to your business. Whip through and identify the obstacles and again do an emotional release on each one.

Notice, there is no limit. Each time you can imagine a way in which your business can evolve further, all you need do is write the goal statement and release any thought or feeling that is getting in the way.

Questions and Answers

At this point you may well have questions, so below I've set out some of the most common ones that have arisen from my clients, together with the answers.

What is the difference between a thought and a belief?

Imagine a table top without legs. The table top represents a thought.

The problem is that the ego has a habit of finding thoughts and attaching all kinds of meaning to them. For instance, say you think that your colleague Rosie doesn't like you. This may or may not be true – but whether it is true or not doesn't matter. The point is that if you let it, your ego will go looking for evidence to back up its belief, whichever decision it has made. Often, if left unchecked, the ego will decide that a negative statement is probably true, and then look to substantiate it. The problem is that immediately we make this decision, we start filtering all incoming information to back it up. Whether we deem this thought to be true or false is therefore not a product of well-analysed data, but of the decision the ego made based on what it thinks will keep it safe.

So, returning to our analogy of the table, if we imagine all the pieces of 'evidence' that the ego brings to our attention to back its decision are the table legs, we can see that these prop up the table top (the thought) and turn it into a belief. So, a thought is just a thought. A belief is a thought with legs on it, that somehow makes it feel more stable and solid.

Our task is to begin unpicking all these subconscious ego decisions, which in themselves are only limitations in our mind and therefore on our world, and start recognizing them as mere thoughts. Once all thoughts are allowed to be equal, we can become increasingly free of these limitations, simply because we don't need to regard them as either true or false. They're just thoughts. If we choose that they mean something, then we are at liberty to make that a conscious decision.

My beliefs are what make me who I am – if I erase them, will I become a different person?

As we've already outlined, you are not your thoughts. Your thoughts come and go, and only *you* remain.

In the same way, the thoughts you choose to hold on to are those that make up the table legs to become beliefs. Your beliefs are merely the product of the decisions you've made when choosing which thoughts to hold on to and which ones to ignore.

This isn't who you are. You can let go of beliefs in the same way as thoughts. And though your thinking and your behavior may alter as a result, your true Self is much more profound than these things. In fact, all the people I've worked with have found that by letting go of their thoughts or beliefs, they have effectively freed themselves up to be more of who they really are, without all the restrictions that past thoughts and decisions used to put them under.

You are a brilliant, amazing person. Letting go of unhelpful thoughts and beliefs doesn't change that. It just allows you to shine more brightly, revealing more of your true Self. And you know who you are. *You* are the essence that whispers words of power and encouragement to you, deep inside in your heart of hearts. You are always safe and always loved.

So changing your mind about one of your obstacles isn't going to change who you truly are, though it may set you free. Try it. (You can always go back if you don't like it!)

'Self' or 'self'?

You may have noticed that when I talk about your true Self I use a capital S. This is to make a distinction between the 'ego' self and your 'real' Self. The ego self is the part of us that demands that we stay safe. It peppers our thoughts with fear and doubt, and causes us to think small and remain unforgiving and petty.

Our true 'Self' (with a capital 'S') is who we really are underneath all the mind chatter and emotional baggage. It's our essence, which is part of the oneness that spiritual teachers speak about. It's the inner voice we hear when we are still that guides us on our path. It's the part of ourselves we are learning to align with, in order to live effortlessly and blissfully following our true purpose.

As you go through your day, try to notice whether your thoughts, feelings, and actions are coming from your true Self or from your ego self.

What about my intentions? Don't I need to put them out into the Universe?

Intentions are the thoughts and feelings that drive the manifestation process. They are not something that needs to be projected outward into the Universe. They aren't necessarily something that you need to focus on every day, unless you're trying to break through some invalid beliefs you haven't released yet. Rather, intentions are a reality and a feeling that you hold already. When you don't hold any baggage around an intention, and you're operating at a high enough energy, the Universe almost shuffles around you to create a continuous field consistent with your intention in the physical world around you.

Let me use a bit of field theory to explain my point. When you were at school, I expect you came across the concept of gravity, which is the force that holds us to the ground, keeps the planets in orbit around the sun, and holds each star in the galaxy on its course. You may even have seen pretty simulations showing that gravity is just a field, like a stretched drum skin, which dips when you put a mass or a finger into it.

For a short distance around that dip, the skin also bends. This drum skin represents what we call the space–time continuum, the four-dimensional 'skin' that we live upon. So, placing a mass in the space–time continuum distorts the field around it, and the gradient (steepness) of the distortion is what we experience as gravity. The steeper the gradient on the distorted skin, the stronger the gravitational field.

Figure 7.1: How mass distorts the field of the space–time continuum

Now, notice in Figure 7.1 that the mass is passive and static, in keeping with the physical laws. Any movement of the planets happens as a result of the varying strength of the gravitational field, which occurs around them naturally as a result of their mass. It's the same with your intention. You hold an intention and the Universe naturally responds in an unseen field, so that the world around you morphs and bends to fit.

How Do I Crank Up My Manifesting Mojo?

An easy way of explaining it is that you become a heavy weight when it comes to making a dip in the manifesting field (see Figure 7.1). How do you do that? By increasing your available energy. This doesn't mean going on a rigorous exercise regime! It means cultivating your high-energy emotions in order to raise your internal frequency, and allowing the low-energy emotions to leave.

High-energy emotions are, of course, feelings of love and acceptance. Courageousness is also an incredibly powerful feeling. It's true what they say about courage not being an absence of fear, but a willingness to step up *in spite of* the fear. In fact, in this way, courage almost marks the move from the destructive emotions (such as fear, grief, greed, and pride) into the positive, high-energy ones.

So to crank up our Manifesting Mojo we hold the intention of staying in our high-energy emotions and allow the lower-energy ones to move out as we let more and more of them go.

You may recall in Chapter 3 we discussed how we become lighter and have more energy available to use when we release emotional baggage. This is where this strategy comes into its own. The more baggage we drop, the more energy we have available to affect the world around us. Not only that, but the more baggage we drop, the more thoughts we release, and so the ones that are left are more powerful simply because they aren't being counteracted by all the negative baggage.

Another thing to be aware of is that the world looks very different when you're vibrating at different energy (or emotional) levels. You may have experienced this yourself: perhaps you can recall a time when you felt very fearful and worried about everything; then compare this to a period when you felt completely happy and at peace with the world. In a state of fear, everything feels risky or even dangerous, but when you're feeling at peace anything seems possible.

So how can we use this insight to manifest more of what we want in our lives? When we release the heavy emotions that are causing limitation, our energy naturally lifts, like throwing sandbags out of a hot-air balloon. At this point we find ourselves more able to manifest what we want, rather than what we fear. Our thinking shifts. Our energy system changes. We find that things that used to bother us, don't anymore. We discover that as we let go of all the emotional and complicated baggage, we relax into a deeper trust in ourselves and the Universe. We start to see everything as intricately interconnected. We see the symmetry of our own minds projected out onto the screen of the world about us. We become more able to take responsibility for creating our world and every detail within it. Remember that our thoughts create our physical experiences in the world.

The physical world around us changes, too. This goes against conventional logic, but when you experience it you'll see for yourself. It's almost as if you start living in an alternative reality where different rules apply. Happy coincidences occur. People who were previously difficult just stop giving you a hard time. Money problems resolve themselves.

What's more, as you can probably deduce, people who occupy high-energy states such as peace and acceptance, are not only more powerful in a congenial and cooperative way, but are happier more of the time. They are also *much* happier more of the time.

Another great thing you will find as you spend more time in the high-energy emotions is that even little increases in energy can have a massive effect on your world. It becomes easier and easier to have things the way you like them, but the trick is to keep releasing the baggage, so that you don't get stuck.

You see, one of things I have noticed is that as soon as things start going their way and their Mojo increases, people have a tendency to stop doing the very things that make this happen. It's like getting really fit, and then sitting back and saying you don't need to go to the gym anymore. The key is to keep setting goals and clearing out resistance, and you'll keep your Manifesting Mojo in tip-top condition.

Force or Flow?

Do you adopt the attitude that it doesn't matter what it takes and whom it hurts as long as you achieve your goal? Or do you opt for only ever being in your Flow and aligned with your own personal Money Mojo? Which do you subscribe to at the moment? Or maybe you're somewhere in between?

Perhaps you recall that when we first discussed the reason for wanting to know our natural Money Genius type, the answer was so that making money could become fun and easy. The fact is that the more you operate in your natural Money Genius profile, the more energy you have available to you, and the more chance you have of raising yourself to a higher energy. You can think about it in very simple terms if you just imagine being in Flow and working to your strengths. This will naturally make you feel happy. Happiness is a high-energy emotion, so just feeling that way lifts your energy and your manifesting power.

We have also already mentioned how *allowing* is such a powerful proposition. In Chapter 7 we ended with an exercise on how to clear out a goal statement in the form: I allow myself to.... This is such a useful technique – and now you probably have a greater sense of why. It can be used all the time to overcome anything you may come across that may be a sticking point, because 'allowing' is a higher-frequency action. It is the opposite of resisting, and the opposite of forcing and struggling. Allowing is higher up the energy scale than other forms of goal statement. There is a certain acceptance in the way we are phrasing the intention and this helps us get closer to realizing it in the material world.

The reason we are using these goal statements and looking for the objections our mind comes up with, is to remove the emotional baggage that is weighing us down and keeping us in fear, anger, or perhaps pride. Each thought we clear out on the issue at hand allows us to drop more of our emotional sandbags out of the balloon, and become lighter and lighter. Each negative thought is a limitation on what we can achieve. The more we drop, the more we push out the boundaries of what is possible for us.

The trick is to keep releasing until you're completely 'clear' on the goal: in other words, until it doesn't matter whether you have the goal or not. As long as you get to the point where you absolutely *can* have the goal, you can stop working on the exercise, and forget about the goal completely. Strangely, after this, it has a tendency to show up and just manifest in your world, and it will seem the most logical and normal thing to happen at that point. This is contrary to the traditional way of achieving goals, in which we are told to write them out and look at them several times a day, as well as to meditate on them. The way we've discussed here is preferable because it also builds our Manifesting Mojo and allows us to release more baggage to feel happier and lighter.

Another thing to notice is that as you let go of the desire to control things, or your feeling of lacking love or of wanting security, you let go of that feeling across every issue in your life. For instance, even though the goal you are clearing may be to do with having a better relationship with someone you work with, or with having better cash flow, or fixing a specific problem, it will have a positive effect on every aspect of your life. What you are doing is releasing the issues that lie at the root cause – within. This means that all the triggers you come into contact with in your external environment will no longer be activated by the baggage. It's like there's no more 'emotional stuff' for these potential triggers to bump up against and set off within you, so the potential issue just evaporates.

When we are operating at a high energy level, we switch into positive, life-giving emotions. We become less driven by selfish or primitive survival mechanisms, as we already feel safe and secure. We don't feel that we need to protect ourselves or make sure we have enough to survive. We're already safe. At this point we become interested in the welfare of others. We want to help and contribute. We deliver more value to society and are able to give more of our Self to the world. We also become more trusting of ourselves and in our abilities. We attempt things despite any negative comments from others around us, and instinctively listen more to the inner voice that guides us. We trust our own instincts and recognize when thoughts or emotional baggage are affecting our judgment. We see thoughts exactly for what they are and are able to let them go. We are brave enough to feel our emotions rather than avoiding or suppressing them. We love – not out of a need for security – but because of who the other person *is*. At higher levels love is a constant state, unconditionally bestowed upon everyone and everything – whether they do what we want them to do, or not. In fact, when we operate in a high-energy state, we find the very concept of wanting something to happen in a particular way tends to evaporate, too.

At high energy it is easy to fall into a constructive cycle: we constantly become lighter and lighter and have more and more energy available for effective action. For all the reasons just outlined, it is also a place where we can release more and more of our emotional baggage more easily. The sandbags just aren't as heavy to haul over the side of the balloon basket.

You may have heard the expression 'gravity is automatic', in the context of driving and developing yourself. It suggests that staying positive is difficult and an ongoing struggle. But at high energy this is no longer a struggle, but a choice. It's much easier. And because you get a taste for how powerful, easy, and fulfilling it is above the line, whenever you find yourself making the choice you'll feel a natural pull to evolve and move up even further.

Now, what we've been doing up to this point is just releasing our baggage from a standing start: from whatever emotional state we happen to be in at the time. Now that we understand the difference between high- and low-energy emotions, and that it is easier to release when we are in a higher state than a lower one, the sensible thing to do would be to get into this state *before* we start working on the releasing exercises that we will continue to do on a regular basis.

How do I get into feeling these high-energy emotions when I'm scared, exhausted, or stressed out?

Great question! And the answer to this is going to mean more to you the more baggage you let go of, and the more you play with the ideas outlined throughout this book. You'll find that you can affect the world around you faster and faster in a positive way, choosing it to be the way you'd like it to be.

The way to get into a higher emotion is simply to experience it right now, in this moment. So, no matter how you are feeling this second, as you read the words on this page, can you just allow yourself to put your feelings aside for a few moments? And as you ignore them, just focus on what it feels like to be really brave. Let's recall the definition of courageousness as doing something, not in the *absence* of fear, but *despite* the fear. So, whatever is going on for you right now, can you just make the decision to feel courageous? And now that you feel a little bit courageous, can you allow yourself to feel even more courageous? And a little bit more? As that feeling intensifies, can you multiply it out, and make it even stronger, and bolder?

By now you're probably feeling so brave that you will have a feeling deep down that no matter what life throws at you, you can handle it. This is because however you feel, you now have a choice and can allow that feeling to leave. And this gives you certainty – certainty that you are safe and in control, no matter what happens in your outside environment. And you probably already realize the reason we hesitate and deliberate is simply because we are fearful of the outcome. But if we can always cope with the outcome, there is much less pressure and we become free to act as we would if fear was *not* driving us.

Now, summoning that feeling of bravery, can you allow yourself to drop any heavy sacks of baggage that may be weighing you down? And by dropping these bags overboard, you'll probably feel yourself drifting into higher energy, up into a place where everything is okay with the world. And now can you allow yourself to feel even more accepting of your world? Can you allow yourself to feel just a little accepting of yourself? And a little more? And even more?

Now can you accept yourself completely? Just as you are – without having to change anything about yourself?

Without having to work on something to make yourself any different from the way you are *right now*? Can you just allow yourself to be as you are? And be okay with that?

If you find that any other thoughts are coming up, just put them aside for a moment – after all, as you already know, a thought is just a thought. It has no intrinsic meaning in itself. And now in this state, you can feel there is no need to do anything. There's no need to change anything from how it is. Anything that needs 'doing' will happen in good time.

And it may be helpful at this point to remember that in nature nothing is rushed and everything is accomplished. This is how it is in your own life. As you feel this acceptance flow over everything that exists, can you realize that there is no difference between acceptance and love. Can you allow yourself to love everything just the way it is? And can you also love your Self exactly the way you are? All is perfect. All is peaceful. You are perfect, complete and at one with the world. And now that you're in this state of peace, can you see how quickly you moved from low energy to a very high energy?

Now that you're in a high-energy state, it would be well worth going back and doing some of the releasing exercises we've already discussed. From this place, you are better able to allow any suppressed emotions to come up and disperse. Go ahead and try one of the exercises now. You'll be amazed at how much easier it becomes.

Done? Great job! Did you notice that all this starts with having the intention to move your energy up into a higher state, a higher level of consciousness?

Are Low-Energy Emotions 'Negative'?

Now the reason I say 'negative' in inverted commas, is to remind us that we don't want to get into the habit of avoiding these emotions. The whole purpose of releasing is to become aware that these emotions are there, and to allow them to come up and leave – to let them go, not bury them deeper, pretend they aren't there, or resist them.

You see, by avoiding them or burying them away, we use tons of energy to keep them locked up. And as we only have a certain amount of energy to invest each day, we don't want to waste 20 per cent of it suppressing emotions we could just as easily let go. So, the trick is to acknowledge and allow ourselves to experience all emotions – whether we term them good or bad from our current perspective – and allow them to come up and then leave.

How Does All This Help Us Manifest Better?

You may have already worked it out, but the higher the energy of the emotions you experience on a regular basis, the more power you have available to create what you want. It's almost as if each of us is an energy battery. We have a finite amount of energy available to sustain our bodies, to plough into our projects, to put into our relationships, and to shift the world around us to make things happen in our favor. Have you noticed how upbeat, loving people tend to experience more happy coincidences than most? This is because they are keeping their energy at a high frequency, and the easiest way to do this is through letting go of as much emotional baggage as you can.

The Manifesting Process:

Based on what we have just discussed, here are some guidelines to get more out of setting intentions and manifesting.

1. Let your first intention be to move up into a higher energy, so that you feel that everything is fine just as it is, then cultivate this feeling so that it becomes super strong.

2. Set your intention. Use an 'I allow myself to...' permission to put the goal into the positive, to minimize the resistance to it, and to put it in the present tense.

3. Add the words 'with ease and grace' onto the end of the statement to remind you that it can be done quickly and easily.

4. Use the grid in Chapter 3 to release any push or pull against this goal.

5. Hold the intention with gratitude as if it's already happened.

Getting More Out of Manifesting

Super-Charge Tip 1: Intentions should be held, not projected

Often when we talk about putting an intention out into the Universe there is a sense that we are sending out beams of light into the space around us. This uses a lot of effort and isn't necessary.

Let's think about our example of a gravitational field again. Recall that a planet, because it has mass, causes a dip or a bend in the space–time continuum simply by its existence there. It doesn't have to send gravitational waves out into the world (although some areas of particle physics assume this approach). The planet just sits there and bends the field around it, causing a greater gravitational field at its surface and a weaker field as one moves further away from the surface.

It's the same for your intentions. The field we are considering when we talk about our ability to manifest is a field that holds everything that exists. It holds our thoughts, our energy system, the physical world around us, the thoughts of others. We can almost say we are sitting in a field of awareness or consciousness. Consciousness is everywhere and interacting with everything, including the physical world. By holding an intention, we are naturally letting it interact with the sea of consciousness.

You need not try and project your thoughts out to another person or place. You are far more powerful when you exist exactly where you are, pulling your energy into the present and allowing the intention to manifest locally, right where you are. What happens then is that just as a planet creates a gravitational pull around it, your intention creates a change in the energetic field around you to make the intention manifest in reality.

In essence, think about holding the intention, rather than pushing it out like radio waves.

Super-Charge Tip 2: Change the Picture

We all hold pictures in our mind about how we think the world is. But because we exist in this field of consciousness, whatever we think creates the world around us. An easy way to change what is showing up in our external world is therefore just to change the pictures we are holding in our mind. This is partly what we do when we set goals, do visualizations, and hold intentions. Change the picture of what is happening, and if you've cleared out the baggage attached to it and raised your emotional frequency, you will find it quite easily becomes real in your world.

Super-Charge Tip 3: Act on Money Ideas Fast

As soon as you get a flash of inspiration, act on it. Ideas that hang around seem to get stagnant and lose their impetus. Acting on them at a later date rarely brings them to fruition. I've found this in both my own experience and when coaching clients. It's almost as if when the time is right, the idea is handed to you. Stay in your Flow and act on it quickly, without letting any baggage get in the way, and you will find the rewards will follow. Remember what we said about Darwin and Wallace, Newton and Leibniz? What if that same idea was handed to someone else at the same time? Get it done and out there quickly – first!

Super-Charge Tip 4: If the Momentum Gets Scary, Keep Clearing

You may have experienced a time when everything really started happening for you, almost as if someone had taken the brakes off and you started flying. However, shortly after this, you may have felt that everything was moving too quickly and you wanted to slow down a bit. With that feeling, you probably energetically or subconsciously put the brakes on your progress again.

Don't worry, you're not alone. We play at the level we're at until we get to the point where we can cope with the next stage. When this happens, we make a jump – sometimes big, sometimes small, but a leap from where we were. Sometimes, we get an opportunity to make a massive leap. In fact, it probably happens more often than you realize. But, if we feel this jump is just too scary, we either fail to see the opportunity, or we sabotage it so it doesn't work out – all so that we don't have to take such a massive step up all at once.

Whatever the outcome, that's fine. But one of the things I've noticed is that often the resistance we experience is just an emotional reaction to the sudden change and the stepping up. So, what if you didn't have that emotional reaction pulling you back during the critical moment? Then you wouldn't be slamming the energetic brakes on every time you got rolling and it's likely you'd rocket from one fantastic success to another!

The fabulous thing is that if you chose to, you could take this emotional resistance out of the equation each time it comes up. How? By using the same emotional clearing technique we've been using. Set the intention of what you'd like to happen, or what you'd like to achieve, even if it scares you. Then fill out the grid (see page 67) to clear out all the baggage around it.

Once you've done this you'll notice that when it's time to make that important phone call, or do whatever it is that is critical for your success, you won't have the same emotional reaction pulling you back anymore. You'll be in full Flow, happy in who you are, as you are, with your Mojo apparent for all to experience!

Points to Remember

- Check your business is aligned with who you are and the things you excel at within your profile

- It is important to be clear about what you want to create

- Eliminate all the baggage that is stopping your truest desires from manifesting

We're ready now to move on to the sixth key, which is all about cultivating and harnessing your power to make money.

Chapter 8
Key 6: Cultivating the Power to Make Money

I like to refer to the seventh key as 'Mojo fodder.' Let me explain. Mojo fodder is the very substance that is going to improve your self-esteem, make you more able to attract money, and give you more power to create what you want in your world. You're now going to learn precisely how to generate more Mojo fodder and maintain a permanent store of it.

Filling the Void

So far we've discussed letting go of the baggage and all the stuff that keeps us heavy and operating at a low energy level. But after all the clearing out, shouldn't we perhaps refill ourselves with some delicious and nutritious food for the mind and spirit? The answer is, most definitely, yes.

But what exactly do I mean by 'delicious and nutritious' in this context? White light? Love? Happy thoughts? In essence, yes. But let me frame it in another way, which fits more easily with the principles we've been talking about. So often we criticize ourselves internally for not doing better, not doing enough, not achieving more. We have fooled ourselves into thinking that this makes us better, sharper, and more productive, but the truth is – it doesn't. In fact, it does quite the opposite.

Disapproving of ourselves ties up huge amounts of energy in our system, slows us down massively, and lets us feel bad about ourselves. It makes us feel like we need to compete with others all the time, and has us making the craziest decisions because we're being run by the false pictures we have in our heads. Without all this drama we would make much better, more constructive, and intuitive decisions.

And this is where the sixth key comes into play. The sixth key is about letting go of disapproval and filling ourselves up with uplifting, loving energy so we can radiate positivity into our lives and allow our true Selves and our intentions to flourish. This, in turn, creates prime ground for cultivating our Money Mojo and getting ourselves firmly into the flow of our Wealth Profile.

How Do We Fill Ourselves Up?

The technique I'm going to teach you now is one of the most fulfilling and helpful you will ever learn. You may have experienced some tricky patches as you've been releasing baggage, most probably when you came up against your ego and your resistance to letting go. Even these difficult times can be made easier by the next exercise we're going to do. Try it just once, and you'll see enough benefit to want to keep going back to it time and again.

Whatever you are feeling right now, can you notice a sense of disapproval for yourself buried in there somewhere? Are you criticizing yourself for something and trying to push yourself to be better? Can you notice this as a sensation in your body? And as you recognize this sensation can you allow yourself to let go of the heavy feeling of disapproval? A little more? That's it. And now can you let go of your disapproval even more, perhaps? Well done! That's great.

Next, I'm going to show you how to give yourself some *ap*proval instead.

Giving Yourself Approval

Now, you know when you feel good, is it because you've done a good job? Or when someone compliments you about yourself or something you've done? It feels good because you're being given approval. (We're using the term 'approval' rather than love, because generally there is a lot of resistance to fully loving ourselves when we first start on this kind of work. 'Approval' is just a little easier for the ego to handle!)

But the trouble with approval is that it is entirely dependent on outside factors. And even if you could set up an environment in which you were always receiving approval from other people, it would become increasingly less satisfying because whilst the ego craves external approval it is simultaneously criticizing you internally, thereby balancing out the approval with disapproval.

Now, when we approve of ourselves internally, we free ourselves from these ego ties, and the more we do it, the less the ego jumps in to criticize us. In this way we can feel better and better about ourselves in a really healthy and productive way, without becoming prideful or trying to control others to give us contrived compliments. We also discover that we don't need to do things or be other than we are in order to gain other people's approval.

So, how about we give ourselves that really good feeling right now: that feeling of healthy self-worth? If you feel you can't give yourself a lot, just start off with a little. So can you now give yourself a small amount of approval? Not for having done anything spectacular, but just for existing. Can you give yourself a little approval just for being *you*? And now, can you feel kind toward yourself? That's great. Can you feel even kinder? And now even a little more?

Sometimes people object at this point, saying that they feel selfish giving approval to themselves – as if they don't think they deserve it. But it's important to know that as you do this, you are actually making yourself a more loving individual. You are cultivating feelings of love that everyone around you will benefit from. You are cultivating the fodder to make yourself less acidic and abrasive toward others. You are making yourself more humane and less judgmental. You are lifting your energy up the scale into more and more positive and healthy emotions. So with that in mind, can you give yourself some more approval? And more... and even more? Well done!

One of the most wonderful things about this concept is that you don't have to do or be anything in particular to 'deserve' approval. The mere fact that you are alive means you are entitled to approve of yourself. Another way to think of it is to ask yourself how you are ever going to be able to love others unconditionally if you can't love yourself in the same way – without strings and without having earned it.

Now, the masters of manifesting using their Mojo have perfected this technique. Several of my highest-flying clients spend several hours a day just sitting without any distractions, giving themselves approval. And this yields massive results for them in their business. They find themselves happier and in more pleasant situations than others who don't do this exercise.

They also find that deals turn out in their favor, their staff flourish, and they attract people and circumstances that are beneficial to themselves and all involved. Life gets easier and more pleasant. Their bank balance swells. They have more fun. Their relationships blossom. Their children learn and grow, and almost seem to adopt their wisdom through osmosis.

Let me tell you about John, who started using this technique to raise his self-esteem about four years ago. At the time he didn't appreciate the huge effect it would have. He was working hard to let go of all the thoughts that were making him miserable and keeping him from making money. As he got better at this, he then began to spend more time just feeling good. In fact, he started spending more and more hours in meditation, just giving himself approval – which directly increased his self-esteem. John spent three or four hours a day just sitting quietly and approving of himself.

It was bizarre to watch over the years as his ability to attract money just rocketed. He started being able to trade the financial markets – not by watching the graphs and using a mechanical trading strategy, but by trusting his intuition and hitting buy/sell at exactly the right time. It was almost as if increasing his self-esteem and self-love increased his intuition and perhaps just as importantly, his ability to completely trust his intuition, without allowing any mental chatter to distract him. As a few more years went by he graduated from trading to bigger financial-market games – moving huge sums of money from one currency to another and making massive profits in a matter of days, all with virtually no effort. The important thing to remember about this story though, is that he didn't start with millions. He worked within his own Money Mojo, cleared out his emotional baggage, and committed to feeling good about himself whether he made a lot of money or not. Feeling good, and approving of himself came first.

Do you think you can benefit in the same way? I believe strongly that you can. Go ahead and put the time aside to do it on a regular basis, and let it become a habit. You won't regret it.

How do we do it?

We simply cultivate a positive feeling of approval and love toward ourselves. To begin with this sometimes means thinking positive thoughts. Notice how you feel when you think good thoughts about yourself. Go ahead – try it now. Feels relaxing doesn't it? Like you've put down a whole load of heavy shopping. Eventually you can just focus on generating this positive feeling without the thoughts. This is how we give ourselves approval.

What exactly are we doing when we give ourselves approval?

In essence we are allowing ourselves the freedom to be exactly who we are. We are relinquishing all the negative energy that keeps us stuck and trapped, and thinking we need to do this or be this in order to deserve that. What we find when we approve of ourselves more and more fully, is that we are absolutely wonderful and perfect just as we are.

What effect does approving of ourselves have on our external world?

For a start we become lighter, happier, and more powerful at creating the world around us as we would like it. It's almost as if we generate more energy to make our intentions manifest. We also increase our self-esteem. This means that we mellow out and don't feel like we need to prove anything to anyone else. People around us find us less spiky or difficult to deal with. People are attracted to us, without knowing why, and will just want to spend more time in our presence.

Cash and Self-Esteem

You will probably have heard the principle that money moves from areas of low value to areas of high value. The more value each of us delivers to the world, or to our marketplace, the more money we receive in return. Using this principle, the common advice offered to attract more money is to deliver more value more often. If you do this, then apparently the Universe will recognize this and automatically reward you for your efforts.

The only difficulty with this is there are lots of very talented coaches, healers, and trainers who deliver outstanding value to their clients, and yet still struggle to increase their income beyond their current levels. It seems to be that just delivering value isn't enough to ensure that we are handsomely rewarded. The missing key to the process is having that value resonating through our system, so that the Universe can actually pick up on the energy field and allow a money–value correction to occur.

In this way, cash doesn't so much move from areas of low value to high value, but instead moves from individuals with low *perceived* value to individuals with high *perceived* value. Think about this in terms of self-esteem and it's easy to understand why self-esteem precedes financial reward.

So, in order to have your Money Mojo activated, it's almost as if you need to cultivate a garden of high self-esteem within your energy field. From here people seem to pick up on your energy field as being one of someone who has a high intrinsic value and is worth doing business with. The Universe also notices it and allows the opportunities to convert value into cash to fall into your lap. On this basis, if you are already delivering outstanding value to your customer base, the next thing to do is some internal work on increasing the amount you value yourself.

The Self-Esteem Map in Chapter 3 (see page 41) works incredibly well. One way in which some of my clients have got even more out of this exercise is by doing it for specific areas they have been struggling with. For instance, one woman had what she thought was really solid self-esteem generally, but was struggling to get her business off the ground. She worked on her Self-Esteem Map focusing specifically on reasons why she should do well in business and she experienced a massive shift soon afterward.

You probably have a particular area of your business or yourself that you'd like to work on, too, to increase your confidence in that area. Some people find it difficult to increase their client fees (particularly if they are in a service-based business). Sometimes individuals feel they lack the ability to stand on stage and speak about their work. Sometimes people need more confidence in communicating with their potential customers, or even in just allowing people to give them money in exchange for their services.

Overcoming a Sticking Point: When You Just Can't Love Yourself

Every now and then it happens. We feel stuck and we just can't approve of ourselves. The simple fact is that most of us on this planet don't really love ourselves. We're constantly told that it's right to love others, but that we shouldn't love ourselves for fear of becoming arrogant and egocentric in the eyes of other people. In fact, this is the biggest lie in the world!

The truth is, the more we love ourselves – really and truly – the less power our ego has, and the less we need to compensate for a lack of love by having a raging ego. When you see people trying to be the center of attention, it's not because they are really confident. It's because they need the energetic input from others to light them up. The more we love ourselves, the more we can get that love energy from our internal, eternal reservoir. At this point, we need never seek approval from anything external to us.

If you have an issue with someone being the center of attention or being adored by other people, check that this isn't a disowned desire or trait within yourself. And whatever you see when you dig deep, know that it's fine, and that you can give yourself some love and approval no matter what thoughts spin around in your head.

So, what should we do if we're getting stuck even just deciding to give ourselves love and approval? The easiest way to deal with this is simply to make the decision to let go of disapproving of yourself. You may need to do this a few times before you succeed in giving yourself some love and approval, but then keep filling yourself up. Continue until another thought or belief comes up, then release it, and carry on filling yourself with even more love and approval. And each time you get stuck, ask yourself: 'Can I let go of giving myself a hard time? Can I let go of being disapproving of myself?' But be careful not to suppress emotions just to feel good, as this is how you get stuck in the first place. If you're feeling good, keep letting go, and allow yourself to feel better and better and better.

Another sticking point we can reach is the jump between being above and below the line separating high and low energy. Recall how, in the last chapter, we talked about having high-energy emotions (such as love, acceptance, happiness, and gratitude), and low-energy emotions (for example, greed, fear, pride, lust, and grief). Now whilst there is a continuum of these emotions, there is an important pivotal point between moving from a low-energy emotion into a high-energy one, where everything changes. Going from low energy to high energy we flip from destructive emotions to life-giving and life-supporting emotions. You may find it easy to imagine it as a scale ranging from deeply negative to extremely positive, with a line, like a foothold or a step, marking the point where you transition from negative to positive.

This line or step represents a movement from pride into courageousness.

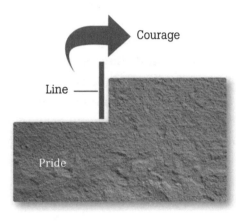

Figure 8.1: The step into courageousness

Pride is the highest-energy emotion of the destructive emotions. It's the first emotion that lets us feel a little bit good about ourselves. In this emotion we find we have achieved something and that makes us feel better than we felt when we were experiencing other low-energy emotions, such as fear and grief. However, pride is still a painful and frustrating emotion. Not only does it hold us back, but when we are prideful or arrogant, and aware that we are being such, it makes us want to kick ourselves very, *very* hard!

The other thing about pride is that (unlike with fear, grief, and anger), when we experience this emotion we are starting to reach a safe place, and as such, we don't attract assistance from others. Arrogance isn't a socially acceptable trait, while fear and grief provoke more sympathy. Prideful energies tend to upset other people. They make them want to put us down a notch or two, because there is something about arrogance that is just plain irritating.

It's only by getting over the dividing line, and stepping up into feeling brave and courageous that we start to open up to new possibilities, and allow ourselves to move up to experience the high-energy emotions. Of course, this takes effort – it's as if we have to climb up a physical step. We have to be prepared to literally step out of our comfort zone and mobilize ourselves. That is why I think of the boundary between the destructive emotions and the life-supporting ones as a step or a dividing line. However, stepping out of our comfort zone is perhaps the last thing we really want to do.

There are a couple of things we can do to overcome this sticking point. Firstly, we can recognize exactly where we are right now. As tough as this is, we don't need to talk about it or tell anyone, just notice it and admit it to ourselves. Secondly, there's the great opportunity to unpick all our self-deprecating thoughts, which won't necessarily be apparent in an obvious way. They will be noticeable in the way we judge other people.

Judgments against others are actually judgments against the disowned parts of ourselves. So, if someone else has a characteristic we particularly judge and dislike, there is a good chance that we, too, have this characteristic, though we may well try to hide it even from ourselves. The trick is then just to keep releasing all the self-critical thoughts and emotions and to cultivate feelings of courageousness. Even when our minds are spinning or trying to hold on to our judgments, all we need do is give ourselves some love and allow our mind to settle, and quietly allow the emotions and resistance to leave.

I've had the pleasure of working one-to-one with a number of clients who are Buddhists seeking Enlightenment. In working with these individuals I have come to understand how learning to love ourselves links up with Buddhist principles and we have shared some fascinating insights. As we've already discussed, self-esteem is fundamental to anything we set out to achieve, whether it is a solid relationship, a small entrepreneurial outfit, or a lucrative multinational enterprise. This ties in perfectly with the Buddhist principle of *Maitri* – loving kindness toward oneself.

This is an incredibly powerful principle. I recall reading an article by Pema Chödrön, an inspiring Buddhist nun, who teaches about *Maitri*. In the article Chödrön described a meeting between His Holiness the Dalai Lama and some Western teachers, who described to him how hard Western students are on themselves. Apparently their pupils would listen to a talk about how we cling to the ego and how hard life can be with all our attachments and desires, and instead of being uplifted and inspired to let go of the ego, they would instead turn the teaching against themselves and become very dismayed. His Holiness was surprised by this reaction, as this does not seem to be a reaction that Tibetan students have.

Chödrön suggests overcoming the problem by cultivating unconditional love for ourselves. In this way, we naturally become more positive and we are less likely to see a snake on the ground where there is only a rope. In essence, developing *Maitri* is the same thing as filling ourselves up with love and approval.

Trust in Your Own Ability

One of the additional consequences of mastering the sixth key is learning how to trust yourself and your own ability: be that your skills, your intuition, or your own judgments when inspiring and organizing your team.

When we add to our internal approval, we are automatically cultivating the ability to trust ourselves. So often we hesitate, hold back, and don't take advantage of an opportunity that drops in our lap simply because we don't feel we are ready for what it entails. Sometimes we don't know what to do in a situation. We wait for that gut instinct or that small intuitive voice in our heads – and it's silent! Or is it? In fact, it's just drowned out with all the mental chatter.

Once you start releasing your emotional baggage, you will find that you are more able to tune out of the ongoing mental chatter, and gradually you will be able to hear the small voice of calm within, which will guide you. But, more importantly, as you increase your internal approval stores you will discover that you act on your intuition more and more. The point to reach is a position where you act on it *consistently*, regardless of how uncomfortable the outcome may be, or how much you have to let go of your previous perceptions of the world, or what you thought your destiny would be. And that's a big ask.

Think of all the things in your life that you are most attached to. Now imagine having to let those go. Until you can take or leave them emotionally, they will still be obstacles that inhibit your intuitive ability, your happiness, and indeed your ability to make more money. The crazy thing is, the less attached to money you are, the less you push it away, and the more readily available it is to you.

In the meantime, the best thing you can do when you hear that inner voice guiding you is to be really brave and just take the next step it is prompting you to take. Get good at taking one step after another and you will come to trust the voice and yourself more and more. And though the prospect of this first step may feel daunting, it gets easier the more you do it, just as lifting weights at the gym becomes more and more effortless with practice. You'll also start to feel healthier and bolder.

When you put down the chains of indecision and fear, and the restrictive illusion that you are not already loved just as you are, you allow yourself to develop the freedom to trust your hunches. Furthermore, you will probably also notice that the more you love and value yourself, the less often you will be inclined to off-load your cash to someone else! You'll become less in need of the next training course or the next miracle cure. You'll become more trusting in your own abilities and will rely on yourself more to achieve what you set out to achieve. When you value yourself highly, there are fewer things you feel compelled to spend money on. You will find that the money sits better with you than it does elsewhere.

When we feel compelled to spend money, it is because we value the person, the product, or the information more highly than the resources we already have. Now, sometimes this is entirely justified. Sometimes you'll come across an expert who knows much more than you and can help you move from where you are to where you want to be. In this case you will find that what you pay them in exchange for the value they offer is fair. However, as you develop and grow, you will discover there are more and more things you realize you *don't* need, because you value yourself and the resources you already have, more.

In addition, your spending on junk food and wasteful items will subside. We often spend money in order to feel better. When you already feel good, you are less inclined to buy something to give yourself good feelings. And as you put more value on yourself, you will find you no longer have such a large void to fill.

The Universe Will Provide for You

As you continue on the journey of creating your world and making your business a great success, it's comforting to remember that it's not your responsibility to think about *how* it's all going to come about.

Your job is to align yourself with your purpose, get into your Money Mojo with your Wealth Profile, set your intention and work on clearing out the resistance. Do what you are compelled to do to reach your dreams: work on them; don't give up; be brave; but then turn them over to the Universe to allow them to happen.

If you take the pressure off yourself, you will find that you naturally do things differently. Take the woman who gave up her name and identity to become known only as Peace Pilgrim. She traveled the world on foot. She took nothing with her: no supplies, no provisions, no companion. She relied solely on the kindness of others and the Universe to provide her food. She slept whenever it was time to sleep, wherever she was, knowing that a safe and comfortable place would be provided for her by the Universe. She circumnavigated the globe in this way, talking to people and journalists along the way, sharing her story. She became a huge inspiration for anyone who heard about her. I've seen her story mentioned in a few places, which leads me to believe that the message she embodied – trust in the Universe as it will always provide for you – was her great gift to humanity.

If you're struggling with this concept, perhaps wondering how it works and how you could possibly surrender and trust as Peace Pilgrim did, it can be useful to go back to our discussion in Chapter 7 where we talked about high and low emotional energy. As we've already discussed, there is a dividing line between the two categories representing where we cross from life-destructive emotions to life-supporting ones.

The world is an entirely different place depending on whether you are operating above or below the line. If you are above the line, you're likely to accept these concepts almost intuitively. They just 'make sense.' There has been no scientifically rigorous discussion of many of these principles (though evidence does exist in the form of other books, texts, and published papers by academics in the field of human consciousness). Readers who operate mostly above the line will take this information on board quite easily and apply it readily.

In fact, you may even use the information in these pages as a kind of rough and ready estimator as to whether you are above or below the line. If these insights ring true and seem useful to you, you are above the line. But if these concepts seem too unbelievable to entertain, you are probably below the line. A person below the line literally experiences a different reality, where logic rules and life is hard, so the principles we have discussed in this book will be difficult to accept. However, you will notice when you set the intention to be above the line and move into the high-energy emotions (see page 196) that the information will be more compelling to you. And with practice you will get above that line.

Now, don't be disheartened if one day you're above and one day you're below the line. Where you estimate yourself to be may fluctuate over time, depending on what emotional baggage is surfacing and being processed out of your energy system. Right now, just ask yourself 'Am I above or below the line?' Then recognize where you are and make the decision to be above the line. Incidentally, this is a great self-coaching question to ask yourself to help you get your Mojo back.

Just having an awareness of where you are gives you the power to choose where you want to be. If you choose to remain below the line, that is a conscious choice. To get above the line again takes only moments and, as we have already found, is the result of merely *intending* to be above the line. It's a conscious decision.

You may want to give it a try right now. Once you recognize you are above the line, go back and read about Peace Pilgrim again and see how you could apply her philosophy to your own quest to uncover your Money Mojo.

Points to Remember

- Fill yourself with light, love, happiness, and joy

- Allow yourself to get stuck now and again, if it happens – you know how to unstick yourself when you are ready

- Let go of any judgments you may have made, both about yourself and others

- Courage is your step up out of fear and low-level energy to higher energies, where making money becomes even easier

- Feeling good is the goal and your key to getting your Money Mojo working again

In the next chapter we will discuss the seventh and last key – the one thing that is still holding you back if you haven't already harnessed you full Money Mojo and achieved everything you desire.

Chapter 9
Key 7: The Activation Step

Congratulations on reaching the last chapter! This puts you in the top percentile of motivated individuals – people who will have the complete set of information with which to complete the process of wiring themselves for wealth. As we've already said, without this final key, the chances of creating real results will be much smaller.

As promised at the beginning of this book, I will, in this final chapter, share with you the one thing that is holding you back. This is the seventh and final key. There are two reasons we couldn't discuss it before this point. Firstly, this final key relies on the other information that has gone before to put it into context. Secondly, it is so simple in its final explanation that it is likely to get lost amongst the myriad other more complex concepts we have discussed along our journey.

Just to recap, so far we have discussed the six keys as follows. You might like to copy these out and pin them up on the wall behind your computer, or paste them into the front cover of your day book or journal, or put them any place where you can constantly remind yourself of them.

Key 1: Increase your self-esteem

Self-esteem is the very foundation of any success. It is the garden with tilled, nutrient-rich soil. We can create and nurture nothing much without self-esteem. But when we have it, projects and progress follow as if by magic, with very little interference on our part.

Key 2: Release your emotional baggage

We weigh ourselves down with so many unnecessary thoughts and feelings, some of which are quite disruptive to our soul and our success. Take the time to unravel the mind tangles, move through the confusion, and in doing so you will naturally allow your true passion *and direction* to shine through.

Key 3: Find your Money Genius type

There is an inscription in the ancient Greek temple of Apollo at Delphi, the home of the famed Delphic Oracle, that advises 'Know thyself.' Knowing where your own Money Genius type lies means that you are working to your strengths and developing your Flow. Remember, the flow of a mighty river is never hindered by a few stones or rocks in its path. So know and develop your Flow.

Key 4: Build your teams with Mojo

This is the most powerful way to leverage your own Flow and to gain maximum advantage by combining it with the Flow of the different Money Genius types around you. If you study any successful person, you'll soon notice that no one ever succeeds alone. Find and nurture your team. Give them a compelling vision. Empower them to take responsibility for the aspects of the projects you entrust to them, and encourage them to increase their own Flow and the combined Mojo of the team.

Key 5: Develop your ability to get results

Develop your Manifesting Mojo by releasing any baggage and increasing the energetic level you operate at – like dropping sandbags out of a hot-air balloon. As we rid ourselves of unnecessary garbage, we free ourselves up to soar higher and higher into our unlimited potential. Become a powerful magnet for positive people, money, and the things you choose to have in your world. You create your world by the thoughts you think and the feelings you experience. Choose the good ones.

Key 6: Cultivate the power to make money

This key complements the strategy of releasing your emotional baggage. Focus on dropping any disapproving, judgmental thoughts and feelings about yourself and others, and generate more and more love, acceptance, and appreciation for yourself.

Each of these keys gives you the tools that will make the difference as you find your Money Mojo and hence will boost your ability to attract more money into your experience. Notice they are called keys. They are not intended to be formulae to create something from nothing. You already have immense value within you. To assume you have to build something from scratch is to deny this incredible value you have and everything you already are. It would suggest that you are somehow lacking. This is not the case!

We are using the keys to unlock the flood gates of your potential, to give you access to the immense power and intuitive genius you already have. You are already whole, complete, and incredibly talented, with a gift to own and bestow upon the world. You are an amazing, worthy human being. You are no more and certainly no less than anyone else around you: in your family, in your marketplace, in your industry, or in your field. You have the same number of hours in each day as any other successful entrepreneur or financial genius. These keys are designed to unlock the same innate potential that any other Money Genius you care to name has already discovered intuitively.

Use the keys. Do the exercises. Not once, but time and time again – as often as obstacles arise or you feel you can't do something. These exercises are specifically designed to free you up, to move you from feelings of 'I can't' to the certainty of 'I can.' You already *can*. So just allow yourself to be in this new reality you are creating every second of your day.

And so we come to the final key. This seventh key is the one most controversial thing I ever suggest in my coaching. It is the one thing that people almost certainly argue about when I first suggest it. But it is always the one thing that gives them absolutely enormous shifts in their businesses, just by accepting it. And so, this is also the one thing you *must* do if you are to master the seven keys and have everything fall into place.

Whichever goal you are having difficulty manifesting, wherever your blockage may be to attracting money, if you have unlocked the previous six locks with the six keys we have already worked through, there is one thing that is still preventing you from reaching your goal. That one thing stopping you from having it is that you still *want* it. Let me repeat that, in case you missed it in the simplicity.

The one thing that is stopping you from having what you want is the fact that you're still wanting it.

It is the wanting that is stopping you from having. That wanting, lacking energy is pushing away your goal. And you are adding power to it every time you feel you don't already have the thing you want.

Remember right at the beginning, we talked about wanting and how it actually means lacking? Remember how we agreed that wanting and having have two very different feels to them? And remember how we learned that the wanting energy is actually the very thing that is pushing our goal away from us?

I took a four-week intensive course with a handful of private clients to work through the aspects of releasing emotional baggage we've been discussing. One of the women was having trouble grasping the effect that wanting has on the things we want. We ended up describing it in terms of relationships. I asked if she had ever experienced a situation in which someone had been really keen on her, but she didn't feel the same about them. She said she had.

When asked if she could remember how the energy of the interaction with that person made her feel, she said it had been uncomfortable, and she didn't want to be around them. 'It felt like a grabbing energy,' she added.

'So what effect do you think you're having on money when you're energetically wanting it?' I asked her gently.

'Oh my goodness, I'm pushing it away in the same way, aren't I?' she replied. The other women gasped as the penny dropped.

So perhaps you now see how you are pulling at whatever you are failing to manifest and making it feel uncomfortable in the same way. Maybe you're trying to force your will onto something and in doing so you are disrupting the natural flow of things. Just notice this energy and allow it to leave. You don't need to make any decisions about what you will do about the situation. Just allow it to *be*, however it is.

I am reminded of a story I've come across a few times on this journey. If you've been in spiritual self-development circles for a while you will probably have heard it, too.

It's the story of a seeker of Enlightenment. Eager to find Enlightenment, the seeker went in search of a sage whom he'd heard had helped countless students on this path. After much traveling and searching he eventually found the sage at a temple and enlisted as one of his pupils.

One day after many months of working diligently on the path, he asked 'Master, how long do you think it will take me to reach Enlightenment?'

The wise old sage considered the question in deep thought, then after a few moments, looked the seeker in the eye and said 'Probably about ten years.'

'Ten years!' the seeker exclaimed. 'But Master, I am prepared to work harder and longer than any other student. I will do whatever it takes to reach enlightenment quickly. I don't think you understand my desire and drive to do this.'

'Ah, perhaps I did not,' replied the sage. 'In that case, it will more likely take you twenty years.'

'Twenty? But Master, perhaps I didn't explain how much I truly want Enlightenment. I'm prepared to do anything to attain it. Just tell me what I need to do – I will show you my devotion to reaching it.'

The amused sage looked at his pupil with love and wisdom in his eyes. 'My child', he said, 'in that case it will most likely take you thirty years to become enlightened.'

And so you see, wanting something is often the very thing that keeps it from our grasp.

Eliminating the Final Want through Gratitude

An excellent way to move out of the field of wanting into the space where something is possible and you have it, is through gratitude. This means you have to learn how to be grateful for any situation and at all times. But how? To become grateful for any situation, you'll need to wade through any feelings to the contrary, so that you become fully accepting of it. Let me explain this in a step-by-step process.

If you have a situation in your business, or in your life in general, that is less than ideal, you still have wanting attached to it. There is still some aspect that you want to be different, or someone you want to control, or someone's approval you need.

Let's take an example – let's say you're in debt. Most people who are in debt are pushing against it and hating the situation. It makes them feel uncomfortable and it is a constant pressure.

The first thing to do is to accept that you have the debt. Include it as part of your experience and your financial growth, and allow yourself to *have* the debt. This will take enormous pressure off and will ultimately help you to clear the debt more quickly and easily. Use the goal grid (see page 166) to clear out all your resistance to having the debt.

The next step is to remove the charge or emotion you are holding on to, which is keeping the debt there. In the same way that you may be resisting it, you are also wanting it and attracting it. So, just as you did with your resistance to the debt, you need to clear out your desire for the debt. Ask yourself: 'What does this debt give me that I might be holding on to?'

You may want to consider here things like: it allows you to hang back from really stepping up your game; it gives you a ready excuse not to invest in yourself or your business and really put yourself on the line; or it allows you to remain the victim, so you don't have to take responsibility. It may even feel comfortable, like a security blanket, because it's been there for so long. Whatever the reasons are, just fill them out on the grid and release them as we have been doing all along. They are just thoughts and feelings that are ready to leave.

You'll notice that what you're doing here is taking out all the wants from the situation. If you've done this effectively you'll accept both having debt and not having debt. Either way you will feel fine.

Once you have done this, the path is clear for you to be really grateful for the situation as it is. What you're doing here is lifting your energy to higher frequencies, thus giving yourself more power to influence the outcome. This is incredibly powerful as you are effectively allowing yourself to become grateful for the situation. You are elevating your feelings to acceptance and then love. In acceptance, all is forgiven. In love we realize there was nothing to forgive and that all is perfect just as it is. Pouring acceptance and love on a situation puts it further within our control, so that not only are we no longer bound to it, but we are also able to influence it from our highest intentions.

Through gratitude you can accept that every situation has come about either to teach you something or to get you into a place, emotionally, geographically, or otherwise, so that you'll be ready for the next stepping stone in your adventure. Why not allow yourself to see the situation as absolutely integral to arriving where you are? It could all so easily have been otherwise. You could have ended up in a different relationship or in a different career, surrounded by a different group of people, and thus you may never have had the experiences you have had and become the person you are today.

The second stage in gratitude is becoming grateful for things you have been working on, in advance of them manifesting, by believing they are already there. As it says in the Bible in the Gospel of St. Mark 11:24:

> *'That is why I tell you, whatever you ask for in prayer, believe that you have received it and it will be yours.'*

And the truth is that the things you have been working to manifest *are* already there – in the making. They are already happening and in play so that you can use them when your time comes. You only need to think of how many people are now making huge amounts of money on YouTube, Facebook, and Twitter, when not so long ago these things didn't even exist. So when those individuals were working in ordinary jobs and slaving away doing something they didn't absolutely love, the very platforms that were required for their massive success were being developed and built. In the same way, as you are reading these very pages now, the platforms for your success are coming into being.

Your task is to stay firm in your intention, be grateful, and increase the energy you have available, which requires you to become fully present in the moment.

Clearing Out the Wardrobe: An Example of Arriving in the Now

I can't count how many times I have heard the same story from various people, myself included, but there is something about the mental shifts that occur when we let go of both internal and external baggage.

You've probably noticed that when one area of your life changes, the rest of your life also shifts up a gear. In the same way, a new project can prompt a de-cluttering of the study, which then spills over to a clearing out a wardrobe, the car, the attic, and the garden. What is happening in these instances is your soul is telling you that you have outgrown the things you feel you need to throw out. It's literally telling you to get rid of the redundant things that are taking up space to allow more good things to flow into your life. After all, you cannot fill up a glass that's already full.

But even more interestingly, when we clear out our wardrobes, particularly the old clothes that we no longer wear because they don't fit, something strange happens. We gain an increased acceptance of who we are as the person who wears the remaining clothes. We no longer have the desire to get back to how we were so that we can wear the clothes that no longer fit. Instead we feel acceptance – as if we've arrived at the place we are in now.

Moreover, we normally become more confident and energetic. It's almost as if the energy that is tied up in the past (when we were able to wear those garments) and the energy that is tied up in the future ('I'll wear them again one day') is now pulled into the present moment. We fully arrive in the now, with excess energy available to plough into whatever project we choose.

So can you see how being fully present is absolutely essential if we are to succeed – particularly if we are at the early stages of a project or business? But this doesn't just apply to the physical wardrobe. Getting your books and finances in order is essential to this end, too; otherwise they will be another drain on your energy.

I've noticed an increase in attracting clients and speaking opportunities following a tidy-up of my own books. What seems to happen is that money flows to areas where it is most organized and looked after. If we're disorganized and don't know precisely what to do with the money when it comes in, it's almost as if we hold it at a distance until we're ready to deal with it. You may notice this feeling at some point when you're quietly letting go of any baggage around money, as this is a common obstacle that arises.

The solution is to emotionally clear the obstacle, using the goal grid (see Chapter 7), so that you realize it is just a subconscious thought, and then put your finances in order to make your money easier to manage as and when it does come in.

Cultivating Even More Results

There are two enormously useful things that are worth recording on our journey toward cultivating our Money Mojo and getting one exciting result after another. They are the things we are grateful for and the things we have manifested as a result of using the seven keys.

Why? Keeping a running log of the things we are grateful for is a way of acknowledging that we *are* grateful, and we *are* focusing on those things. And remember, our mind is creative – whatever it dwells upon it creates more of, whether we do it consciously or unconsciously. If we keep a log of the things we are grateful for each day, we find ourselves thinking of them and finding other things to be grateful for. As we do this, our thoughts create more instances in our world to be grateful for and so we have more positive things to dwell upon. Try it every night before you go to bed and you'll be amazed at the difference it makes to your world.

The other fabulous thing about getting into a habit of being grateful is (as we've already mentioned) that it's an excellent way to keep your Mojo energy high. It feels better and more empowering, and it gets far more promising results than being at any lower emotional energy level. Check it out and give it a go for yourself. Once you see what a difference it makes in your world you'll want to keep going!

It is also a good idea to record all your results and successes from using the seven keys. Long after you read this book, the things you make happen as a result of using the seven keys will stay with you. In fact, one day you will forget that they were ever a 'success.' They will feel normal and part of your world – as if they have always been there. But, more importantly, you'll have forgotten how you made them happen in the first place! You'll think it would have happened anyway and your mind may even try to convince you that you were just lucky.

Keeping track of your results as a consequence of using these seven keys is also valuable because it keeps a record of what you have achieved and how you did it. This means that you'll be able to create the next things you choose to manifest in your life with ease, simply by following the successful formula again. There is no wheel to be reinvented. It becomes merely a case of making sure your goals are aligned with your purpose; deciding how you want your life to be; discovering your personal Money Genius type; and then clearing out any emotional baggage that may be in the way. After that all you have to do is be as grateful for the result as if it has already happened. The record is a reminder for your mind of the process you used.

I've noticed that if my coaching clients stop keeping a note of their results, they tend to forget that it was letting go of the baggage that allowed them to manifest the result. They then get sucked back into the world at a lower energy level, where things are hard work, where life is tough, and only the lucky get the breaks. All of a sudden the deals stop happening, the list of customers dries up, and cash flow becomes something that needs managing very closely. When they come back to using the principles and keeping a note of their results, they start playing above the line again, and everything falls into place effortlessly.

So, it is a choice. Now you know. *You have a choice.* Do you continue to do things the way you always did, and perhaps continue struggling and battling with the outside world, (but what you now know is really your inner Self)? Or do you choose to let life flow, for business to be easy, fun and effortless, and always to let go of any baggage? I hope you choose the fun and lucrative route, because I know you have the power and the genius within you to make anything you choose possible.

And remember as we said at the beginning of this chapter: You are already whole, complete, and incredibly talented, with a gift to own and bestow upon the world. You are an amazing, worthy human being. You are no more and certainly no less than anyone else around you: in your family, in your marketplace, in your industry, or in your field. You have the same number of hours in each day as any other successful entrepreneur or financial genius.

So why not *you*? Why can't you do it, too? To your unlimited success!

Points to Remember

- There are seven keys to wiring yourself for wealth

- Clear out and get rid of anything in your life that doesn't serve you: possessions (including your wardrobe), circumstances, and people

- Eliminate wanting and lack through showing gratitude

- Become grateful for your financial situation as it is and then for your goals before they have manifested

Afterword

I sincerely hope you have enjoyed reading this book. Those who do all the exercises not just once, but again and again are those who will reap the most benefit. My heartfelt wish for you is that you, too, will gain massive rewards from the time you've invested in reading it.

Remember – if you haven't already – take the time to find out what your profile is (see www.wireyourselfforwealth. com for further resources), so you can fully embrace those traits that make you able to excel at specific tasks. This information will help you increase your success rate and reduce your work-rate, no end.

Also, please feel free to claim all your free bonuses associated with the purchase of this book from my website. As I can't be with you in person when you read the book, you will benefit greatly from having the additional audio tracks. They talk you through the process and give you live examples of the exercises covered.

I would love to connect with you and hear all about your successes. Please do contact me via Facebook and one day perhaps I'll have the honor of meeting you at a seminar or a workshop.

Until then, my friend, take care, and live life more boldly. To your unlimited success!

Laura Leigh Clarke

Recommended Reading

What follows is a list of books that I personally recommend. These books have a permanent place on my bookshelf and have helped me on my own journey. They are packed with wisdom, knowledge, and insights that are well worth absorbing and taking with you on your own journey. I hope they will find their way onto your bookshelf, too.

Bolton, Robert and Dorothy Grover (1996) *People Styles at Work: Making Bad Relationships Good and Good Relationships Better*, New York: AMACOM

Burchard, Brendan (2011) *The Millionaire Messenger*, New York: Morgan James Publishing

Demartini, Dr John F. (2004) *How to Make One Hell of a Profit and Still Get to Heaven*, Carlsbad CA: Hay House

Gladwell, Malcolm (2002) *The Tipping Point: How Little Things Can Make a Big Difference*, London: Abacus

Godin, Seth (2008) *Tribes: We Need You to Lead Us*, London: Piatkus

Hawkins, David R. (2002) *Power vs. Force: The Hidden Determinants of Human Behavior*, Carlsbad CA: Hay House

McTaggart, Lynn (2007) *The Intention Experiment: Using Your Thoughts to Change Your Life and the World*, New York: Free Press

Myss, Caroline (1997) *Anatomy of the Spirit: The Seven Stages of Power and Healing*, New York: Bantam

Twist, Lynne (2006) *The Soul of Money: Reclaiming the Wealth of Our Inner Resources*, New York: W. W. Norton & Co.

Resources

More information about Laura's work can be found at:
www.lauraleighclarke.com
   Email: contact@lauraleighclarke.com
   Press enquiries: press@lauraleighclarke.com
   Speaking enquiries: speaking@lauraleighclarke.com
   To connect with Laura:
   www.Facebook.com/lauraleighclarke
   Visit www.wireyourselfforwealth.com for additional
and supporting resources, including free, guided-release
meditations specially created for the reader.

JOIN THE HAY HOUSE FAMILY

As the leading self-help, mind, body and spirit publisher in the UK, we'd like to welcome you to our family so that you can enjoy all the benefits our website has to offer.

 **EXTRACTS** from a selection of your favourite author titles

 **COMPETITIONS, PRIZES & SPECIAL OFFERS** Win extracts, money off, downloads and so much more

 **LISTEN** to a range of radio interviews and our latest audio publications

 **CELEBRATE YOUR BIRTHDAY** An inspiring gift will be sent your way

 LATEST NEWS Keep up with the latest news from and about our authors

 **ATTEND OUR AUTHOR EVENTS** Be the first to hear about our author events

 **iPHONE APPS** Download your favourite app for your iPhone

 HAY HOUSE INFORMATION Ask us anything, all enquiries answered

join us online at **www.hayhouse.co.uk**

  292B Kensal Road, London W10 5BE
T: 020 8962 1230 E: info@hayhouse.co.uk

ABOUT THE AUTHOR

Laura Leigh Clarke is a money coach to individuals and small business owners wanting to make more money and attract more clients. As a physics graduate, she spent the first part of her career turning around the sales departments of a number of UK companies, and now helps entrepreneurs do the same with their businesses. Laura uses wealth profiling, emotional releasing techniques, and good business blueprints to help coaches, consultants, healers, and therapists make more money by implementing proven strategies and changing their internal relationship with money.

Laura also writes for *Network She* magazine, and has been a guest on BBC Radio, Andover Sound, Star FM, and On FM, to name but a few. As well as speaking professionally at business growth groups around the UK, Laura also runs workshops and a highly successful online money mentoring group for solopreneurs building their own platform and following.

www.lauraleighclarke.com